PLAINS INDIAN AND MOUNTAIN MAN ARTS AND CRAFTS:
An Illustrated Guide

Written and Illustrated

by

CHARLES W. OVERSTREET

Eagle's View Publishing
A WestWind, Inc. Company
6756 North Fork Road
Liberty, UT 84310

Library of Congress Number: 93-74239
ISBN 0-943604-41-9

First Edition

10 9 8 7 6 5 4 3 2 1

TABLE OF CONTENTS

ACKNOWLEDGMENTS

First, I thank my wife Dorothy, for her love and help with editing during the writing of this book. Every writer needs a good editor and I have the best.

Also many thanks to my many Indian friends who were so kind and helpful in sharing their heritage with me. Without their able assistance, this book would still be an idea. I am fortunate to count these men and women as friends. Names like Walking Stick and Red Shirt mean little to the reader, so I'll just mention their tribal affiliations: Cheyenne, Pawnee, Apache, Kiowa, Arapaho, Crow, Ute, Comanche, Lakota Sioux and Minniconju. My brothers and sisters, I love you and thank you!

Many men and women from the following museums were very helpful in researching this book; too many to mention by name. I thank each and every one who gave me so much help.

         Black Kettle Museum, Cheyenne, OK
         Center of the American Indian, Oklahoma City, OK
         Culture of the Plains Indian Museum, Canon City, CO
         Denver Art Museum, Denver, CO
         Davis Gun Museum, Claremore, OK
         Gilcrease Museum, Tulsa, OK
         Indian City, USA, Anadarko, OK
         Kiowa Tribal Museum, Carnegie, OK
         National Cowboy Hall of Fame, Oklahoma City, OK
         Oklahoma Historical Society Museum, Oklahoma City, OK
         Panhandle Plains Historical Museum, Canyon, TX
         Plains Indian Museum, Cody, WY
         Quanah Parker Center, Cache, OK
         Southern Plains Indian Museum, Anadarko, OK
         Woolaroc Museum, Bartlesville, OK

ABOUT THE AUTHOR

Charles Overstreet was born in Cherokee, Oklahoma. Son of a cattle rancher, grandson of a homesteader in the Cherokee Strip land run; his roots run deep in Oklahoma's red earth.

At an early age he developed an appreciation and love for the American west and Indian culture. Many characters in his writing reveal a work ethic and moral code he learned from his father and other men of his youth; cowboys, ranchers and Indians.

After graduation from Oklahoma A and M College, he served four years in the Army as an armored officer. Following a tour of duty in Korea, he entered the advertising business. His career in advertising agencies and corporate advertising took him to Iowa, Oklahoma City, New York and Los Angeles. He also traveled in the Orient, Europe, Canada and South America. After 25 years in business, he accepted a professorial appointment at Oklahoma State University where he teaches several advertising courses.

He and his wife travel extensively throughout the Great Plains, Southwestern and Mountain states visiting historical sites, conducting interviews and researching events in the great libraries and museums of the West. His writings, both fiction and non-fiction, are based on historical accounts of the mountain men; their lives, adventures and interactions with various Indian tribes of that period.

INTRODUCTION

Before one can truly appreciate and understand the Plains Indians and their culture, a certain amount of research is necessary.

Prior to the time the white man came to the plains and the Rocky Mountains, the Indians enjoyed the fruits of unquestionable freedom. It is difficult to think of this part of the United States void of highways, electric power, telephone lines and fences. It was a wild, beautiful, wide open country interrupted only by rivers, mountains and forests. The inhabitants loved their home and roamed the vast country as truly free men and women.

When the first white traders, trappers and hunters entered the domain of the Indian they were accepted as friends. After all, the Indian had little to fear from these few lone adventurers. True, they looked strange with their pale and hairy faces, but they were friendly and for the most part didn't impose themselves on their hosts. Respect from both sides cemented relationships that lasted for years. Many Anglos moved into and out of Indian lands with total freedom and no fear. Some married Indian women, participated in all phases of Indian life and fought alongside their tribesmen against all enemies. A few rose through the ranks and attained the honored position of war chief.

This period, in the mind of the author, was the shining times of the mountains and plains; white men learned the Indian culture and Indians learned from their white counterparts. No hidden motives or false pretenses, every man was accepted by others exactly as he was, no questions asked.

It was not until the white man became selfish and wanted more than the Indians were willing to give that trouble started. There never were great numbers of Indians but the white men were counted as blades of grass or stars in the sky. History sadly tells us of the terrible outcome.

But as you read this book and construct these projects, think of the shining times when Indians and whites lived as brothers. These few short years represent an era of which we can all be proud.

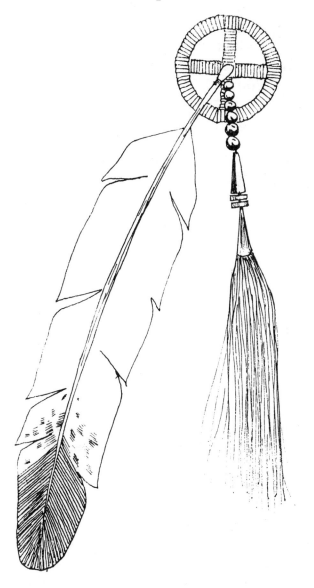

7

MAKING RAWHIDE

One of the most versatile materials used by the Indian and mountain men was rawhide. It is an important component of many of the projects in this book. It may be obtained from leather and craft stores, but it is easy to make and many craftspersons prefer to make complete projects, down to and including materials needed to manufacture the items.

Rawhide is untanned leather and when wet it is extremely flexible and easy to cut and sew, much the same as cloth. When it dries, it takes on its most endearing quality; it shrinks and becomes quite strong in its binding power. Strips of this material work like wire, but with one important advantage: During the drying process, the shrinking gives added strength to the item being constructed or mended. Mountain men repaired broken rifle stocks with rawhide; some claimed the stock was stronger after the restoration than before. Indians used rawhide to secure handles to war clubs, for lashing lodge poles and for drum heads, moccasin soles, parfleche containers and mending broken items.

Rawhide can be made from any type of animal hide. Since the craftsperson usually finds many uses for the material, it is suggested larger animal hides be used in making rawhide. Indians and mountain men usually used buffalo, but deer, elk, moose, steer, mountain sheep, goat and horse hides make excellent rawhide.

Materials Needed

1 Fresh hide
1 Graining pole
1 Scraper, graining tool or butcher knife
1 Drying frame
1 50' small rope or twine
1 50 gallon plastic or wooden barrel
       with top removed
1 5 pound bag of dehydrated lime
1 Pair Rubber Gloves
1 Quantity soft or fresh water

Work should commence as soon as possible after the hide has been removed from the carcass; the same day, if possible. It is best if the hide has not been salted or treated with chemicals.

The first process is the removal of the hair. Place enough water in a wooden or plastic barrel to completely cover the hide. Do not use a metal container. The chemical used is caustic and will rust the container and discolor the hide. Rain water or soft water is best, if available. For every 6 gallons of water, add one pound of dehydrated lime. Stir vigorously as the lime is added. Wood ashes were used in this process and do a good job, but sometimes lime is easier to find and works quite well.

Place the hide in the solution and let soak for 4-5 days; longer in cool weather. Stir the hide each day to assure the entire

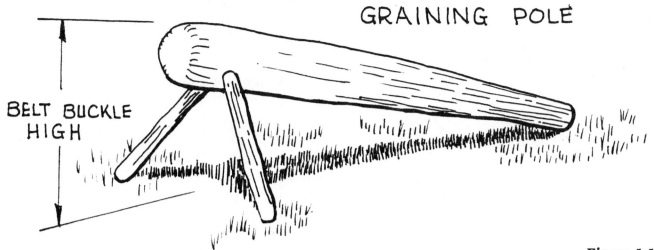

GRAINING POLE

BELT BUCKLE HIGH

Figure 1-1

hide is treated with the solution. After 5 days, test to see if the hair "slips" off. If it does, it's ready to continue with the process. If the hair does not "slip" easily, leave the hide in the solution another day or two. Be sure to wear rubber gloves when working with the solution; lime water tends to dry and crack the skin on the hands. The gloves also protect any small sores or cuts that may be on the hands. Direct, unprotected contact with the de-hairing solution should be avoided. If an accident occurs, wash the area thoroughly with fresh, clean water and seek medical assistance.

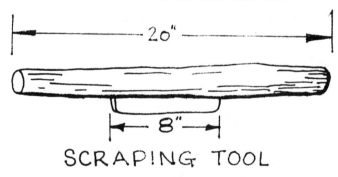

20"

8"

SCRAPING TOOL

Figure 1-2

Construct a graining pole, using an 8" round fence post or log approximately 8' long, as shown in *Figure 1-1*. Elevate one end of the pole to waist level and remove all bark and sharp edges. Round the working end of the pole as indicated in *Figure 1-1*.

Scraping tools are easy to make with a hardwood handle and an old file (see *Figure 1-2* and *Figure 1-3*); all measurements are

approximate.

If *Figure 1-2* is preferred, cut a slot in the bottom of the wood selected for the handle. Insert the file into the slot leaving about 1/2" of the file projecting from the bottom of the handle. Then grind off the sharp end corners of the file.

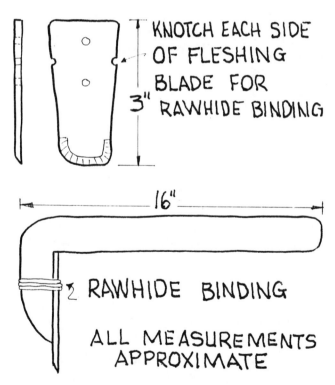

KNOTCH EACH SIDE OF FLESHING BLADE FOR RAWHIDE BINDING

3"

16"

RAWHIDE BINDING

ALL MEASUREMENTS APPROXIMATE

Figure 1-3

If the scraper in *Figure 1-3* is preferred, it is made by grinding a piece of 1/8" iron to a sharp edge and attaching this to the

9

handle with two screws or rawhide lacing. Either works great and provides a scraping tool that lasts a lifetime.

Figure 1-4

When the hair "slips" easily, remove the hide from the de-hairing solution and place it on the graining pole, hair side up as shown in *Figure 1-4*. Using the scraping tool, scrape the hair off by pushing the tool away from you. Be careful not to rip or cut the hide during this process. De-hairing is rather messy, so, if desired, spread a tarpaulin or like ground cover under the post and wear an apron during this step. There is a lot of hair on a white tail deer, so don't forget to find a suitable method of disposing of the waste.

Figure 1-5

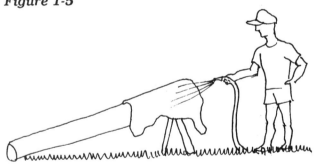

When all of the hair has been removed, turn the hide over and scrape all flesh and animal fat from the hide. Work slowly and keep the hide moist; much care must be taken to keep from cutting the hide. The amount of flesh residue left on the hide depends on the skill of the skinner. The more care taken during removal of the hide from the carcass, the easier this job will be. This waste will be disposed of along with the hair.

After the fleshing is completed, wash the hide thoroughly with water; both sides must be cleansed. Flushing it with a water hose works best as illustrated in *Figure 1-5*. Use plenty of water during this process as the hide must be completely free of the lime-water solution.

Attach the hide to the drying frame as shown below in *Figure 1-6*. If working in the summer, place the frame in a shady place and never in direct sun light. The hide should dry slowly and placing it in the sun will cause it to dry too quickly.

When the hide is completely dry, remove it from the drying frame. The material will be stiff and care must be taken to store it properly until it is ready to use. A good method is to drive a small, headless nail on the inside wall of a garage or storage shed and hang the hide on the nail by one of the holes used on the stretching frame. Insure that the rawhide hangs flat on the wall.

Drying Frame

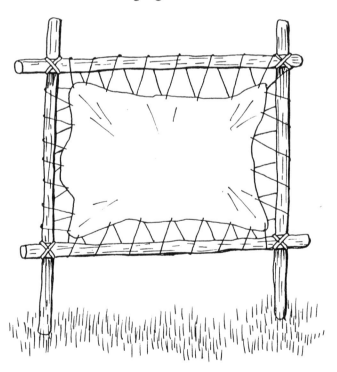

Figure 1-6

TANNING LEATHER

Tanning an animal hide not only preserves it, but turns the hide into a workable material from which many things can be made. Hides are converted to leather by first removing the fur, or if a pelt is desired, the hide may be tanned with the hair intact. When properly tanned, the material remains soft, pliable and odor free for years.

There are as many formulas for tanning leather as there are people who tan. The author has tried many and found the one presented here to be the best and easiest to use. The good thing about this formula is that it will not over tan and it contains no acids or poisonous chemicals. Tanning leather is neither a nice job nor an easy one and to do a professional job requires a lot of time and effort.

Materials Needed
1 Fresh hide
1 Wooden or plastic barrel
1 Plastic 3 gallon bucket
6 Pounds of salt
2 Pounds of powdered alum
1 Hardwood paddle
1 Plastic trash bag

To prepare the hide for the tanning solution, all animal fat and tissue must be removed from the flesh side of the hide. If leather (material without hair) is desired, the hide must be de-haired. Instructions for these processes are outlined in the *Making Rawhide* chapter beginning on page 1 of this book.

After the hide has been prepared for tanning, the tanning solution must be mixed. Always wear rubber gloves when working with this solution; although it contains no toxic chemicals, it is hard on human skin and contains a lot of salt which hurts should it get into a small nick or cut on a finger.

Use a large plastic or wooden barrel as a tanning vat and a plastic bucket for mixing. Do not use metal containers as the solution will rust them and may stain the hide being tanned.

Add six pounds of regular table salt to 10 gallons of warm, soft water. Rain water works great if it is available. Pour the salt in slowly, constantly stirring with a wooden paddle to assure the salt completely dissolves in the water. A paddle such as the one shown in *Figure 2-1* is a good choice and can easily be made from a piece of yellow pine.

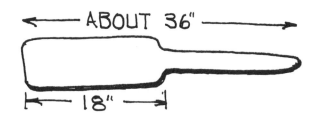

ABOUT 36"

18"

MAKE PADDLE OUT OF 1 x 4 x 36 INCH YELLOW PINE

Figure 2-1

Next, in a plastic bucket, mix two pounds of alum in enough hot water to completely dissolve it. Then combine the salt and alum solutions, stirring with the paddle to assure the tanning solution is completely mixed. The temperature of the tanning solution is not important, except that it should not be used while hot.

Place the hide to be tanned in the solution, making sure that the entire hide is submerged. Large hides may take more than 10 gallons of tanning solution - if the hide is not completely covered, mix more solution and cover it. Gently stir the hide in the solution twice a day with the wooden paddle. To successfully tan a hide, the solution must reach every crevice, fold and wrinkle of the hide. Check daily to assure all areas are being soaked by the solution. A rabbit hide takes about two days to soak completely through; a deer hide takes about a week.

After the hide has been in the solution for several days, carefully use a sharp pocket knife to cut off a small piece near the edge. If the color is uniform all the way through the material, tanning is complete. If there is a difference in color between the two outer surfaces and the inside of the hide, return it to the solution for another day or two. Check each day, using the same method and when the color is consistent throughout the material, the hide is tanned.

When the tanning process is complete, remove the hide from the solution and rinse it completely with a garden hose, as indicated in *Figure 2-2* or in a wash tub. If a tub is used, change the water several times while rinsing. All tanning solution must be rinsed out of the hide at this time.

After the solution has been rinsed out, hang the hide, fur side up, on a rope, clothesline, or suspended board as shown in *Figure 2-3*. During this period, the hide must be kept out of direct sunshine and air must be able to circulate around the hide, inside and out. Keep it out of reach of the family dog; he would love to chew on it!

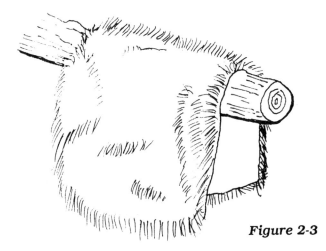

Figure 2-3

In three or four days, while the hair and hide are still slightly damp, fold the hide, flesh side to flesh side, and roll it up in a tight roll as illustrated in *Figure 2-4*. Let the hide set overnight, again protecting the hide from neighborhood pets. If time slips away and the hide dries before it can be rolled, simply dampen a sponge and use it to wet the flesh side of the hide. When the hide becomes pliable, roll it up as just described.

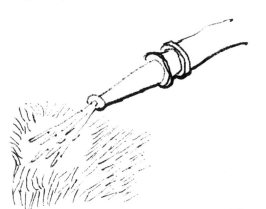

Figure 2-2

Figure 2-4

Now comes the hard work. Unwrap the hide and work it by stretching it, pulling it over a smooth edge such as a rope (see *Figure 2-5*), and twisting it by hand. The purpose of this is to make the leather workable by breaking down all the fibers using these techniques. Indian squaws were charged with this duty and they chewed hides with their teeth to soften them; this is definitely not recommended. It's hard work and takes a lot of time, but this is the most important step in the whole process. It helps to keep the hide slightly damp while breaking down the leather.

Figure 2-5

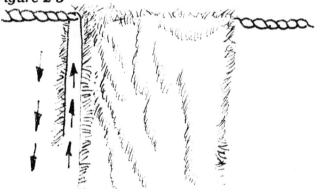

PULL MATERIAL BACK AND FORTH OVER A TIGHTLY TIED ROPE TO BREAK THE NATURAL FIBERS AND SOFTEN THE LEATHER

After the leather is soft and pliable, use hands and fingers to rub in a good leather oil. Neat's foot, cottonseed, and corn oil all work well. Using warm oil speeds up this task. Be sure the oil is rubbed in to all areas of the flesh side of the hide.

If the hide was tanned with the fur, it may contain some dirt, be matted and look pretty ugly. Fill a plastic trash bag with hardwood sawdust. Put the hide in the bag, tie the bag shut and shake for about thirty minutes as shown in *Figure 2-6*; this should remove all of the dirt from the fur or hair.

Shake the hide hard and remove as much of the sawdust as possible. It will shake off the flesh side fairly easily, but the hair or fur may need brushing or combing to make it attractive.

The hide is now leather and will last several years. It may be used to make many of the projects in this book, or it may be used to make a throw rug or a wall hanging.

Bear skins make beautiful rugs and wall hangings. The leather is extremely durable. Beaver skins make warm coats and wear well. Calf hide leather is used to make slippers, wallets, purses, etc. Deer skins are soft and pliable and also wear very well.

Indians and trappers used leather and fur pelts to make gun covers, possible bags, belts, knife sheaths, winter coats, and much more. The craftsperson will find many uses for leather and take pride in knowing the entire project was made from scratch.

Figure 2-6

MAKING BRAIN-TANNED BUCKSKIN

Buckskin is a wonderful material. Indians and mountain men used it almost exclusively for all their clothes. Buckskin is not tanned with chemicals as is most leather, but is preserved, made pliable and soft as velvet merely by a lot of rubbing which breaks down the natural fibers of the hide. It sews easily and makes tough, strong moccasins and warm, windproof clothing.

Brain tanning was the ideal way for the Indians to preserve the material. When a deer was killed, the carcass contained all the ingredients necessary to brain tan the hide; it could be converted to buckskin on the spot!

It takes little talent to make good buckskin but it does take desire and a lot of hard work. If the craftsperson follows these directions, takes the time necessary and wants to build their muscles, he or she will be rewarded with a beautiful piece of soft buckskin.

Materials Needed

1   Fresh deer hide
1   Graining stick
1   Hide frame
1   Three gallon plastic bucket
1   50 Ft. 3/16" or 1/4" rope
1   30 Ft. strong string
1   Large harness needle
1   Quantity animal brains

To prepare the hide for brain tanning, the hair must be removed and all animal fat and tissue must be removed from the flesh side of the hide. Instructions for these procedures are given in *Making Rawhide*, beginning on page 1 of this book. Extra care must be taken in preparing the skin for buckskin; all hair follicles must be removed as well as the outer layer of skin just under the hair (the epidermis). This process results in both sides of the finished buckskin having a suede finish. A great deal of time and effort is required to prepare the hide properly. If all the hair follicles and epidermis are not removed before the brain mixture is applied, the solution will not be able to penetrate properly and ugly dark spots will appear on the finished buckskin.

The next item needed is some brains. Deer brains work fine, but if they aren't available, the butcher in the local supermarket is certain to have some on hand. Calf or pig brains are inexpensive and work just as well as deer brains. Be sure to purchase fresh or frozen ones; canned or processed ones will not work. If they are frozen, allow them to completely thaw. Add about 1 1/4 pounds of brains to a little hot water. Use a potato masher to pulverize the brains into a thick paste. A blender, if available, is ideal for this process.

Rub this paste into the hair side of the hide. Continue rubbing with the palm of the hand until the hide is almost dry. Continue this process until the entire hide has received the treatment.

Then place the hide in a plastic bucket with enough warm water to cover all of the material. Wash and rinse it around in the bucket by hand. The water will become foamy as if the hide was being washed with soap. Capture a pocket of water in the hide and squeeze it through the material. Continue this process until the water squeezes through the hide quickly and easily. The entire hide must receive this treatment.

Remove the hide from the bucket and wring out as much water as possible. Stretch the hide tightly on a drying frame as shown in *Figure 3-1*.

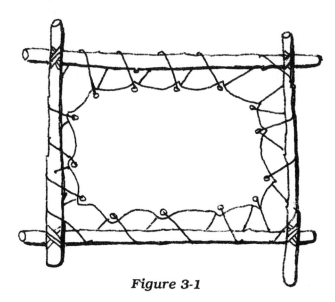

Figure 3-1

Place the frame in a shady place (do not work the hide in direct sunlight) and start to work with a breaking tool such as the one illustrated in *Figure 3-2*. Use the breaking tool to rub the hide, covering every part of both sides of the hide. Fast work is needed for this process, as is the use of a lot of muscle. Spend more time on the hair side than on the flesh side, but keep rubbing hard until the hide is dry. This rubbing process gives the soft, velvety quality to the hide.

If the hide is not soft enough, dampen the hide again and continue rubbing. Another method which works is to remove the hide from the frame, dampen it, and pull it back and forth around a smooth post. Pull

as hard as possible until the hide is dry. A lot of labor is required to break down the natural fibers, but the end result is well worth the effort.

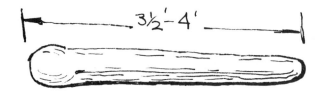

HARDWOOD BREAKING TOOL

3½'- 4'

ROUNDED AND SANDED CORNERS

Figure 3-2

The last step is smoking the hide. Smoking gives the material a rich, golden hue, closes the pores, toughens the buckskin and waterproofs it. Use a set-up similar to the one shown in *Figure 3-3*.

SEW HIDE INTO A BAG & HANG OVER SMOKE HOLE

USE PEGS TO SECURE HIDE AROUND SMOKE HOLE

Figure 3-3

First, use strong string to sew up the hide so it resembles a sack, leaving one end open. Then dig a small hole in the ground and build a fire in the hole, as depicted in Figure 3-4. Add white cedar or willow chips to smother the flame and make a smoky smudge. Hang the bag over the hole and use wooden pegs to secure the hide tightly around the hole. Sometimes a couple of short sticks may be needed to help keep the bag spread open.

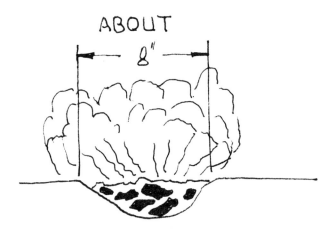

ABOUT 8"

DIG A SMALL FIRE PIT
AND BUILD A SMOLDERING
FIRE - ADD WHITE CEDAR
OR WILLOW CHIPS TO
CREATE SMOKE

Figure 3-4

Stay with the hide as it smokes. Take a peek every few minutes to make sure the fire does not rekindle. Too much heat will ruin the hide. Keep checking and when the desired color is achieved, turn the hide inside out and smoke the other side for about the same amount of time or until both sides are about the same color.

Rip the sack open, fold the hide up tightly and put it aside for a couple of days to cure. Later, wash it thoroughly with soft water to remove the smoky smell. Hang the wet hide on a clothesline and allow it to dry. If the buckskin becomes stiff when it dries, simply work it between the hands and it will quickly become soft once again.

The material is now ready to make war shirts, breech cloths, moccasins or a hunting jacket.

PLAINS INDIAN BEADWORK

The Plains Indians liked to decorate their clothes as well as all their accouterments and weapons. In the early days, they used porcupine quills, carefully dyed with various natural elements, for this purpose. But this type of decoration was greatly diminished after the white traders introduced glass beads as trade items. The glass beads offered brighter colors and were much easier to use. The sophistication of the designs increased significantly and the new art form spread across the plains. Some of the most beautiful beadwork to be seen anywhere is found at the Buffalo Bill Plains Indian Museum in Cody, Wyoming. Everyone interested in beadwork should visit and view the work displayed there. Several of the projects discussed in this book have beaded decoration, thus this chapter is necessary to complete those projects.

Materials Needed

1 Loom
1 Beading needle
1 Sheet of 1/8" square draft paper
  Linen thread, well waxed
  Seed beads of various colors
  Colored pencils corresponding
    to the colors of the beads

The first step in beading is to find or create the design to be crafted. A little research before the design is started pays tremendous dividends. Several books are available at local libraries which give the craftsperson much needed information. Each tribe was known by the manner in which their clothes were crafted and decorated - every tribe had their own designs.

A pattern for the chosen design should be made on graph or drafting paper. Each square represents one bead. The finished beadwork should follow the pattern drawn, but it will not be exactly like the pattern as the beads are wider than they are thick. Beading graph paper is available and if it can be found, the pattern will more closely match the finished piece. Either way the paper design is useful because it gives a working plan to follow.

A simple loom is needed to make beaded belts and headbands. Most hobby shops have such looms but some crafters may wish to make their own and they are simple to construct.

To make the loom shown in *Figure 4-1*, use pine or hardwood for the base and hardwood for the uprights. The dimensions suggested can be varied based on the desired size of the finished beadwork. Use wood glue and wood screws to secure the uprights and make sure the glue is dry before using the loom. Use finishing nails on the ends for securing the warp threads. Care must be exercised when cutting the small slots for the thread. These tiny slots, 1/16" apart, are best made with a sharp Exacto knife blade, but watch the fingers, because sharp blades can make nasty cuts!

Always use well-waxed linen thread when

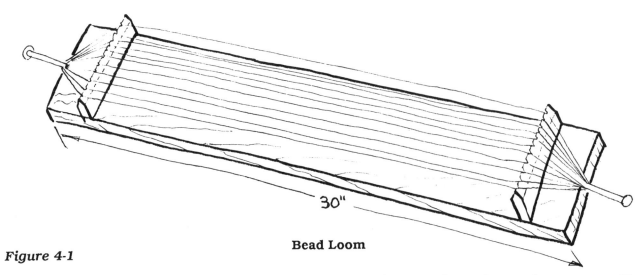

Figure 4-1

Bead Loom

doing beadwork. To string the warp thread, tie the end to one of the finishing nails and start in the middle. Go around the second nail and string the first warp thread to the left of the center. Go around the first nail again and string the first warp thread to the right of center. Continue in this manner, working out to the sides until all the threads are strung. Stretch the warp threads as tightly as possible on the loom, then wrap the end around the nail and knot securely. There must always be one more warp thread than the number of beads. To make geometric designs always use an odd number of beads. For example, nine, eleven, or twenty-one beads gives an equal number of beads on each side of the center line of beads.

To bead, place the loom so that it

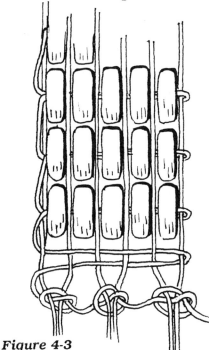

Figure 4-2

extends away from the craftsperson. Start working on the far end of the loom and work towards the near end. Thread the beading needle with about 18" of thread and tie the end of this bead thread on the left side of the warp threads. Bring the bead thread under the warp threads (to the right) and place the first run of beads on the needle. Slide the beads down on the bead thread and position them under the warp threads. Use a forefinger to set the beads in their proper places (between the warp threads). Run the needle back through the beads. Make sure the bead thread runs over the warp threads on this second pass. Then go under the warp threads and repeat this process until the design is finished. This procedure is illustrated in Figure 4-2.

To secure the threads at the end of the design, weave the beading thread over and under the warp threads, from side to

Figure 4-3

side and then knot it around the warp threads as shown in *Figure 4-3*. This procedure can also be used at the start of the piece or adjacent warp threads can simply be knotted together. Just be sure the ends are secure.

Opaque beads usually make the prettiest designs, but transparent beads may also be used. Browbands are usually about 1 1/4" wide and require at least twenty-one beads per row. Usually loomed beadwork is sewn to a backing of cloth or leather with the warp threads tucked underneath.

The design dictates the number of beads between stitches. When the design calls for straight lines, there may be as many as six or eight beads of the same color, as in *Figure 4-4*. Whenever the color of the beads changes, there should be a stitch. On curves, a stitch should be made after every two or three beads as shown in *Figure 4-5*. When moccasins are beaded, the beading receives a lot of abuse and each bead should be stitched down separately as illustrated in *Figure 4-6*.

The Sioux of the northern plains per-

Figure 4-4

If the craftsperson wishes to apply beads directly to buckskin, different techniques are used. The first is called the overlay stitch and is suited for curves. It was used by Woodland tribes as they fashioned their floral designs. The second is called the lazy stitch and is suited for straight lines. It was used by the Plains tribes for their geometric designs.

When executing the overlay stitch, two threads are used. The beads are strung on the first (bead) thread and the second (sewing) thread stitches the bead thread to the buckskin as shown in *Figure 4-4*. Start by inserting the sewing thread through the material, then string six to eight beads on the bead thread. Use the sewing thread to stitch the bead thread to the material and then string more beads on the bead thread. The sewing thread does not go all the way through the buckskin, but should run just below the surface of the material, under the beads.

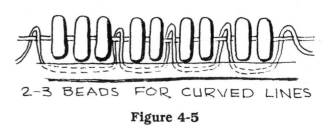

Figure 4-5

Figure 4-6

fected the lazy stitch to reduce the labor required for their geometric designs. Their designs had no curves making this simpler technique possible.

To start the lazy stitch, attach the end of the thread to the buckskin and string about six beads to it. Then stitch the row of beads into the buckskin. String the same number of beads on the thread and bring it parallel to the first row and make another stitch as shown in *Figure 4-7*. The design is built up of rows of beads (horizontal and vertical) attached only at the ends of each row as illustrated in *Figure 4-8*. After a vertical row has been completed, further rows can be added horizontally to complete the design. On the lazy stitch, pull the thread tight so that the beads bulge or arch outward a little as shown in *Figure 4-9*. This gives a beautiful pulse to the beading and easily identifies it as Plains Indian work.

Beading needles are fragile, so use an awl to perforate the buckskin before making the stitches. Again the thread does not go all the way through the material, but runs beneath the surface. Care must be exercised when using either the overlay or the lazy stitch. If the thread is pulled too tight, it will pull out of the buckskin; a few failures will indicate the correct pressure to use.

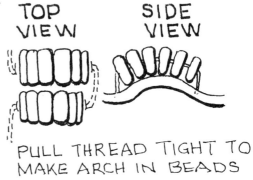

TOP VIEW   SIDE VIEW

PULL THREAD TIGHT TO MAKE ARCH IN BEADS

Figure 4-9

TOP VIEW

Figure 4-7

SPREAD BEADS TO MAKE DETAIL CLEAR

SIDE VIEW

Figure 4-8

It takes lots of practice to accomplish good beadwork. Take the time required to learn and much enjoyment can be had reproducing this great art form.

THE KIOWA ANTLER-HANDLED AWL

A bit of knowledge about antlers is helpful prior to starting on this project. Bucks shed their antlers each year after the annual rut, or mating season. New growth is larger and usually a tine or prong appears each year. The outer surface of an antler is hard, tough and durable but has a porous and softer core.

Mountain men and Indians made many useful items from the horn of the buffalo and other members of the bovine family. A horn differs from an antler; it is a hollow sheath covering a bony core that grows on the skull of the animal. It is permanent and grows larger and longer as the animal matures.

Both antlers and horns are similar in their capacity for being altered by man. They are both relatively soft and quite workable. They may be sawed, filed, sanded, drilled, carved and polished. One of their most endearing qualities to the craftsman is that when boiled in water they become soft and pliable, allowing for re-shaping into the desired shape. Yet, as the material dries and cools, it retains all of it's original strength. Indians excelled in their ability to work with antlers and they often split and straightened elk antlers to make bows with tremendous power.

Antlers are found on White Tail Deer, Black Tail or Mule Deer and Elk. White Tail Deer have the smallest antlers with the most delicate curvature, while Elk antlers are the largest and grow significantly longer and heavier.

There are a great number of projects that may be made from antlers, and many are covered in this book, but the awl is illustrated and described here because it is used in making many of the projects that follow.

One of the first items needed for working with leather is an awl and the one described here is a replica of the one used by Kiowa women. The awl is easy to make and can be completed in an hour or two.

Materials Needed

1 Piece of deer antler about 1 1/4" in length
1 Large, heavy harness needle
1 3" piece of choke cherry or other suitable
        wood approx. 3/8" in diameter
   Quick drying epoxy cement
   Sand paper and steel wool
        Varnish, stain or paint, if desired

Select a piece of antler near the corolla or near the first "Y" (see *Figure 5-1*). The larger the diameter of the handle, the easier the awl will be to use. After sawing the antler to the proper length, approximately 1 1/4" in length, round off all of the sharp edges with a file and then sand thoroughly using finer and finer grades of sand paper, ending with 600 grit as shown in *Figure 5-2*. Do not file or sand the sides of the handle as this will destroy the beautiful, rough and natural texture of the deer antler.

Figure 5-1

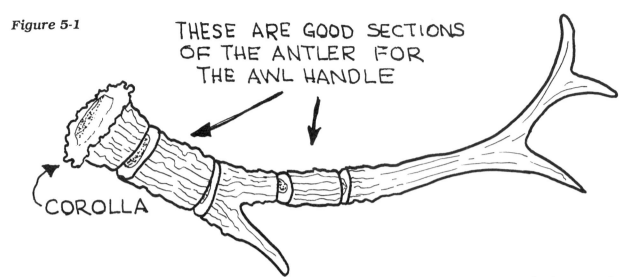

THESE ARE GOOD SECTIONS OF THE ANTLER FOR THE AWL HANDLE

COROLLA

Figure 5-2

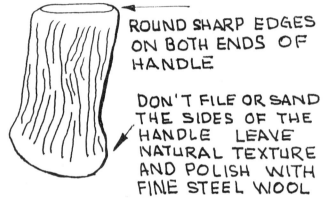

ROUND SHARP EDGES ON BOTH ENDS OF HANDLE

DON'T FILE OR SAND THE SIDES OF THE HANDLE LEAVE NATURAL TEXTURE AND POLISH WITH FINE STEEL WOOL

Finally, carefully polish the handle with a fine steel wool. The awl is used quite a bit when working with leather and a smooth handle is much easier on the hand. Take plenty of time in this process as the handle takes on a beautiful ivory-like appearance when polished. Some museums display awls that are fantastic works of art, many with delicate scrimshaw designs on the butt end of the handles.

When the sanding and polishing is com-plete and the handle feels comfortable against the heel of the hand, drill a hole in the small end of the handle about 1" deep (*Figure 5-3*). This hole should be slightly larger than the diameter of the harness needle to be used. The needle should slide in and out easily, but with no "slap". The slight difference is needed for the epoxy to bond the entire length of the needle and hole to give a secure bond.

Figure 5-4

INSERT HARNESS NEEDLE INTO HOLE — USE 2-PART EPOXY TO SECURE NEEDLE

DRILL HOLE FOR NEEDLE IN CENTER OF ANTLER HANDLE

Figure 5-3

Mix the epoxy as per the instructions and grasp the needle by the pointed end. Roll the eye end in the epoxy (*Figure 5-4*). Make sure the first 1" of the eye end gets a liberal coating and insert the eye end of the needle into the hole made in the handle. Be sure that the needle is seated in the bottom of the hole. Wipe off any excess epoxy and set the awl aside until sufficient time has passed to allow the epoxy to set.

The awl can be a dangerous instrument and should be handled with care. Indian women made a sheath to protect the point and save themselves the agony of stab wounds when reaching into a parfleche box or sewing bag. This sheath is made with a 3" piece of choke cherry or willow limb. Using the same drill bit used above, drill a hole in the center of the piece of wood about 2" deep (*Figure 5-5*).

Making sure that the epoxy used on the awl has cured, insert the awl into the sheath and push it in slowly, bit by bit until the awl seats itself completely into the sheath. When the awl fits snugly, the sheath should not fall off of the tool. Sand the sheath carefully to eliminate all sharp barbs and edges. The

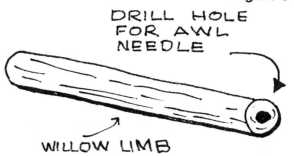

Figure 5-5

DRILL HOLE FOR AWL NEEDLE

WILLOW LIMB

sheath may be decorated with painted designs, stained and oiled or simply oiled in its natural state. A coat of linseed oil will enhance the appearance of the handle and protect it from the elements.

This tool will serve its purpose for many years, but if it should become dull, a stone will bring the point back to its original sharp condition. Remember, the sharper the point, the easier the tool is to use. Also keep in mind that a sharp needle point makes a nasty wound. Be sure to use care when handling or working with an awl.

ACCESSORIES

The Plains Indians were a vain people and liked to dress themselves in beautiful clothing adorned with many types of decoration. The utility or use of clothes was not enough; to enhance an item with feathers, beads, etc. made it special to the owner and admirable to his/her friends and associates. Almost every thing made was treated as special and decorated in some manner. They used natural things or objects that were easy to find in their environment. Some items were obtained through trade; Anglo traders brought beads from the east; before these were available, Indian women used dyed porcupine quills to embellish various items.

SEA SHELLS

Since the Indian's only methods of transportation were either walking or the use of a horse, it is difficult to understand or believe how they traveled such great distances. But they did travel; they followed the Pte (the Sioux word for buffalo) as the great herds roamed the prairies. They traveled to steal horses, capture slaves, hunt, fight and sometimes to trade with other tribes.

When peaceful meetings between various tribes led to trading, new items were brought in from other cultures. As an example, sea shells were used by Plains Indians to decorate many items although there were no sea shells on the prairies. The shells came to the plains by way of tribes who traveled great distances to trade.

If a craftsperson desires to use shells as ornaments, they are easy to find and use.

Materials Needed

1 Package of sea shells
1 Small (1/16") metal cutting drill bit
1 Hand operated drill

If a craftsperson does not live near the ocean, hobby shops are an ideal place to locate sea shells; select those which are pleasing to the eye.

Carefully, drill one small hole in each shell. Remember that shell is fairly fragile and will break if too much pressure is used when drilling. Drill slowly but deliberately. A metal cutting drill bit is recommended as a wood bit dulls quickly when used on calcium shells. Electric drills are not recommended as they run too fast and tend to break the shells before the hole is complete.

It is also a good idea to place a little water on the shell while drilling as this helps keep the shell and bit from getting too hot.

After all the shells have been drilled, simply sew them on the garment as indicated in *Figure 6-1*. Women often decorated dresses with row upon row of sea shells.

SEW SHELLS ON APPAREL WITH STRONG THREAD

Figure 6-1

24

HOOVES AND DEW CLAWS

The Indians were a frugal people; when they killed game, they used everything the carcass had to offer. All the meat was used, including brains and tongues; stomachs became water pouches and cooking pots; intestines were used to store meat for winter, much like sausage; bones were used for knife handles and tools; hides were used for lodge covers and clothes; even hoofs and dew claws became decorative, sometimes religious totems.

Hooves and dew claws are hardened hair follicles which are pretty ugly until properly finished. But when scraped, filed and sanded, they take on a bright, shiny appearance and are beautiful to behold.

Hooves and dew claws were used to decorate clothing, war shields and buffalo lances, to name only a few. In addition to their religious significance, they represented the superior hunting abilities of the owner and were highly prized decorative pieces.

Materials Needed

4 Legs from a Mule or White Tail Deer
Finishing materials

Cut the hooves from the leg bones at the joint located just above each hoof. The dew claws come off the leg bone easily with a sharp knife. Use extreme caution when using the knife, a simple slip can cause a nasty cut.

Fill a two pound coffee can with water and place it on a fire. When the water boils, drop the hooves and dew claws in the water and boil them for a couple of hours. Keep watch on the water level and add water as needed so that the water does not boil away and ruin the hooves.

Use a pair of tongs and needle-nosed pliers to check the hooves after a couple of

hours. Be careful when doing this; boiling water can cause terrible burns. When flesh, gristle and sinew slip from the hooves, take them out of the water and pull everything out of the hoof shells. The hooves and dew claws will be extremely hot, so take care in handling them. When this process is complete, place the hooves and dew claws in a safe place (pets love to chew on them) where air can circulate around them and allow them to dry for several days.

Now comes the difficult job. It takes a lot of time to scrape, file and sand the hooves and dew claws, but the more time and labor spent, the more beautiful the end result.

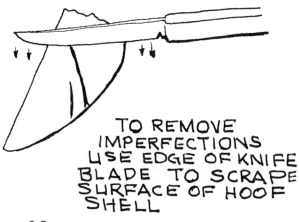

TO REMOVE IMPERFECTIONS USE EDGE OF KNIFE BLADE TO SCRAPE SURFACE OF HOOF SHELL

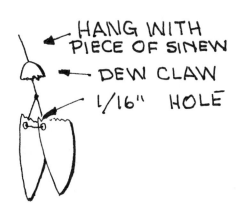

HANG WITH PIECE OF SINEW
DEW CLAW
1/16" HOLE

Figure 6-2

Figure 6-3

Because deer sometimes run over rocky terrain, there may be some deep scars in the hooves, as illustrated in *Figure 6-2*. These are removed by carefully scraping the surface around the scar with a sharp knife; sometimes a wood file also works well. When these scars are removed, sand the items thoroughly and continue sanding with ever finer grits, ending with 600 grit, wet or dry paper. Do the final buffing with extra fine steel wool.

These totems were usually sewn on items or strung on a leather thong. Use a 1/16" bit to drill one hole in each hoof and dew claw (*Figure 6-3*).

Use these items as decorations for other projects in this book.

ANTLERS

Possibly no other article was utilized more for decoration or had more varied uses than deer antlers. They served as buttons, pendants and beads for neck- laces, and toggles to hold parfleche closed. Uses for antlers are limited only by the imagination of the crafter, so only those mentioned above are discussed here.

Materials Needed
1 Antler
Saw, drill and bit, and finishing materials

Antlers may be hard to find, but if the crafter lives in deer country a deer hunting friend may be the best source. First determine what is to be made and proceed as directed in this section. Begin by cleaning the antler completely with steel wool. Hard rubbing creates a beautiful patina and is highly recommended.

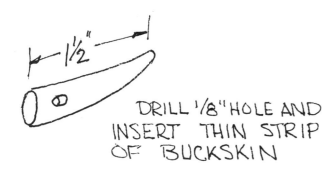

DRILL 1/8" HOLE AND INSERT THIN STRIP OF BUCKSKIN

Figure 6-4

It is best to start with toggles since they are made from the tip of the antler. Saw off the tip, about 1 1/2" long and drill a 1/8" hole in the largest end of the tip as shown in *Figure 6-4*. This hole is needed to secure the toggle to the item. A loop is also attached to the item, which the toggle then passes through, forming a secure lock (see *Figure 6-5*). Sand away the saw marks from the butt end of the toggle and it's complete.

TO CLOSE SLIP TOGGLE THROUGH LOOP

Figure 6-5

Small beads come next and are made by sawing 1/8" thick cross sections from the antler. Remove the saw marks with sand paper and drill a 1/16" hole in the center of

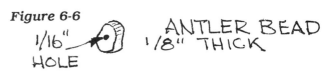

Figure 6-6

1/16" HOLE

ANTLER BEAD 1/8" THICK

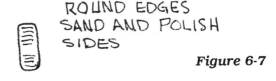

ROUND EDGES SAND AND POLISH SIDES

Figure 6-7

each bead as shown in *Figure 6-6*. When removing the saw marks, it is best to round the sharp edges of the beads slightly as illustrated in *Figure 6-7*. Antler beads are most beautiful when mixed with other types of beads and laced consecutively by size as in *Figure 6-8*.

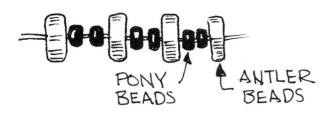

Figure 6-8

Buttons come from larger sections of the antler and are made much the same as beads. Depending on the job the button has to do, it may be advisable to cut the cross sections slightly thicker, but no thicker than 3/16". When the saw marks and sharp edges are removed, drill two 1/16" holes near the center of each button (see *Figure 6-9*). Large buttons may expose the porous inner antler; this material is softer than the outer portion and care is needed when drilling the holes. If desired, cover the buttons with a single coat of epoxy to give them added strength.

ANTLER BUTTON

Figure 6-9

A large cross section of antler makes a beautiful pendant for a beaded necklace. An oblique cross section, as shown in *Figure 6-10*, gives an interesting shape and is

usually prettier than a plain round section. Drill a 1/16" hole at one edge, then insert and tie a short piece of sinew through the hole. Use this sinew loop when lacing the pendant on the necklace.

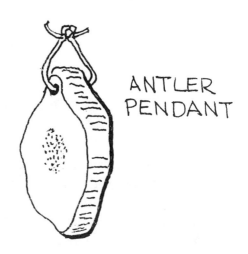

Figure 6-10

Mountain men sometimes wore bandana-like cloths around their necks and used a section of an antler as a kerchief slip. Such a slip is easy to make and quite attractive. Cut a 1/2" cross section slab from a large diameter (at least 1 1/4") antler. Remove the saw marks and sharp edges, then drill a 3/4" hole through the center of the antler, as illustrated in *Figure 6-11*. This hole should remove all the porous center of the antler, leaving the hard outer portion only. Use a rat tail file to smooth the edges of the hole and the slip is ready to use. Some mountain men slips were wider, up to 1 1/2" and adorned with beautiful carvings of animal figures.

ANTLER BANDANA SLIP

Figure 6-11

TINKLES

Another decorative item used by the Plains Indians were tin tinkles. Like sea shells, some women sewed row upon row of small tinkles on their dance dresses. The small tin cones, when sewn close together, made pleasing tinkling sounds and apparel so decorated was much desired by Plains Indian women.

Materials Needed

1 Tin coffee can
   Tin snips, needle-nosed pliers,
   solder gun and solder

Remove both ends from the coffee can, cut it lengthwise and flatten the tin. Most cans are made with strengthening ridges so a smooth area must be selected and removed for use. Width of the material used should be about 1 1/4" wide; measure and scribe lines as indicated in *Figure 6-12*.

LAYOUT TINKLE BLANKS ON TIN MATERIAL AS SHOWN

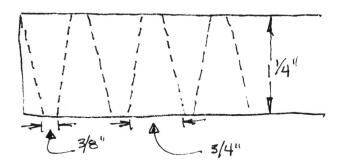

Figure 6-12

SLOWLY BEND TIN AROUND LONG NOSE PLIERS UNTIL EDGES MEET

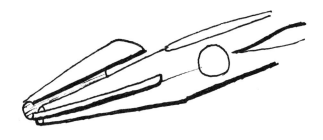

Figure 6-13

SOLDER JOINT

Figure 6-14

Cut the tinkle blanks from the tin and use needle-nosed pliers to bend the cone to shape as shown in *Figure 6-13*. Solder the edges of the cone where they come together; the finished cone should have an opening on the small end (see *Figure 6-14*).

To sew the tinkle on material, about 3/16" of the small end must be smashed together in a vise and a 1/16" hole drilled through the flat area. The tinkles may also be attached to the ends of fringed leather.

In this case, simply insert about 1/4" of the fringe into the tinkle and smash the end of the tinkle with a pair of pliers. Regardless of the manner of affixing the tinkles, they should be placed close enough together so they can make "magic music" when the wearer moves.

Tinkles were used only on ceremonial apparel, never on everyday, hunting or warring clothes.

BEADED FEATHERS

Eagle feathers were used to decorate almost everything. Since they are no longer available, local hobby shops provide suitable substitutes in the form of dyed or painted turkey feathers. They come in a variety of colors and are perfect for decorative uses on all Indian artifacts.

The feather must be smoothed by fingering it from the quill to the outer edge. Every feather has built-in zippers that hold it together. Fingering, using the fore finger and thumb connects these "zippers" and makes the feather look full and complete.

If fluffies (also called feather fluffs) are desired, attach three to the quill, just below the feathered portion. Use glue and a small tie wrapped around the quill as indicated in *Figure 6-15*.

Next, glue a 3/8" x 4" piece of soft leather to the bottom portion of the quill and wrap the leather with thread as shown in *Figure 6-16*. Notice how the leather loops around the tip of the quill.

Next, wrap a piece of 1 1/2" x 2 1/2" felt around the quill and stitch up the back (see *Figure 6-17*). Finally, apply rows of beads to the felt as illustrated in *Figure 6-18*.

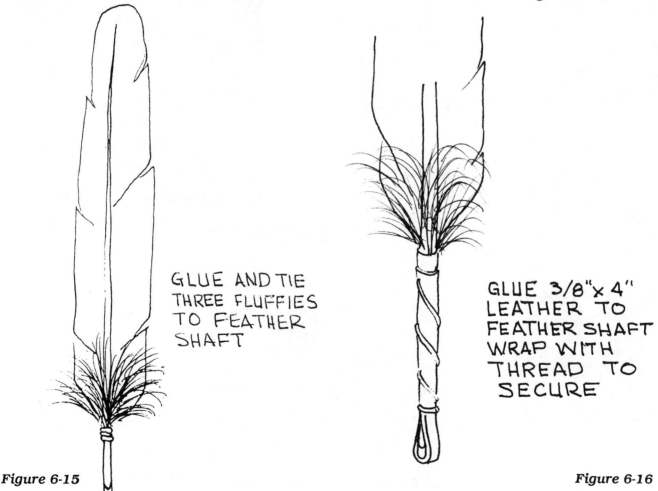

GLUE AND TIE THREE FLUFFIES TO FEATHER SHAFT

Figure 6-15

GLUE 3/8" x 4" LEATHER TO FEATHER SHAFT WRAP WITH THREAD TO SECURE

Figure 6-16

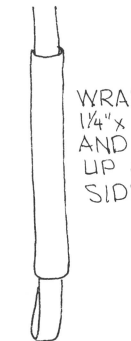

WRAP WITH
1¼" x 2½" FELT
AND STITCH
UP ON BACK
SIDE

Figure 6-17

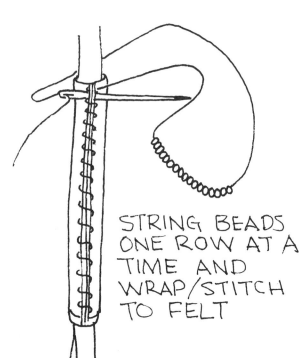

STRING BEADS
ONE ROW AT A
TIME AND
WRAP/STITCH
TO FELT

Figure 6-18

Seashells

Deer Hooves

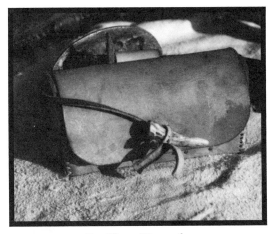

Antler Toggle

Antler Beads

30

Buttons

Antler Pendant

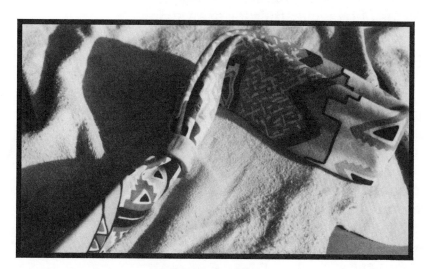

Bandana Slip

Feather

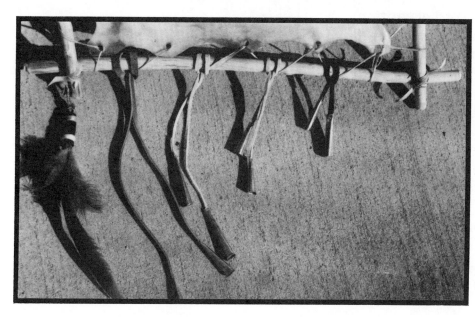

Tinkles and Feather

31

MOUNTAIN MAN BALL BAG

There were many items made and used by the mountain man; some were used in his occupation of trapping beaver, and others were necessary for his convenience, security and safety. His ball bag, used to carry lead balls for his rifle, was an item prized by the trapper and was never far from his reach. The fifty caliber rifle was one of the most popular sizes and took a strong, well-made leather bag to do the job. This project is a reproduction of that type and size bag.

Materials Needed

1 12" Square piece of elk or heavy buckskin
1 36" Piece of sinew or imitation sinew
2 18" Strips of heavy leather for drawstrings

To begin, select a piece of elk leather or heavy buckskin approximately 12" square. The pattern (see *Figure 7-1*) represents one side of the bag and two sides are needed for the project. It is recommended that the leather be cut into two pieces approximately 6" by 12", sandwiched together so that both sides are cut at the same time. This assures that the two pieces match and fit properly when sewn together. Do not worry about cutting the fringe at this time; that will be the last step of the project.

Use an Exacto knife with a new, sharp blade to cut the leather. A word of caution: Cutting leather properly takes a very sharp knife and extreme care must be taken during the cutting process. Do not try to cut through both layers of leather on the first pass and take plenty of time during this step; several passes may be necessary to complete the task. Be sure to use a cutting board of soft wood to save the point of the cutting instrument and the top of the work bench.

The line of dots shown on the pattern represents the awl holes needed to sew the two halves of the bag together. Use the pattern as a rough guide to punch the holes

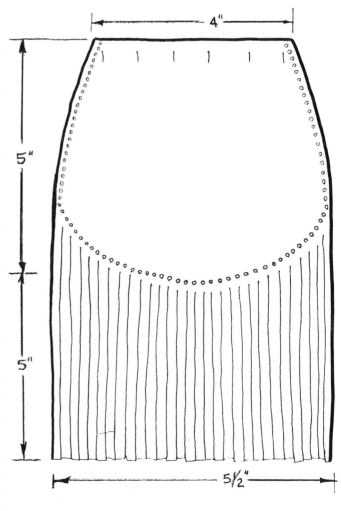

Figure 7-1

as indicated (approximately 3/16" between holes). Again, the two sides are sandwiched together for this operation so that the holes match to facilitate the stitching procedure.

Figure 7-2

Saddle Stitch

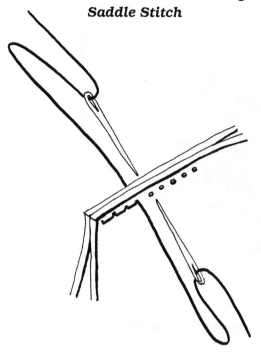

Using the saddle stitch, sew the two sides together using two needles and sinew as illustrated in *Figure 7-2*. Pull each stitch snug as it is completed. However, be careful and consistent as pulling the stitches too tight will cause the leather to "pucker" and become unattractive.

After the stitching is completed, secure

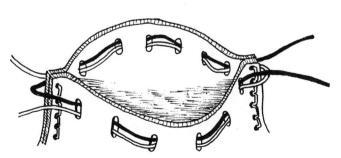

Figure 7-3

the ends of the sinew with a strong knot. On the pattern, note the six small slits near the top of the bag. If these cuts have not already been made, do so now. Insert the leather drawstrings through these slots; both are needed to close the bag securely (see *Figure 7-3*).

Figure 7-4

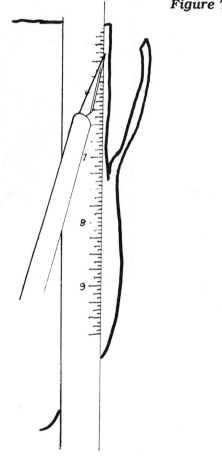

Place the bag on the cutting board and, using the Exacto knife, cut the fringe on the bottom of the bag. A metal straight edge is a handy tool to use in this operation; it will assure neat, straight lines as the fringe is cut as shown in *Figure 7-4*. Take plenty of time and watch that sharp blade! The bag is now complete.

Ball bags came in all sizes and shapes. Some were plain while others were decorated with bead or quill work. Plain trappings were made for everyday use, but decorated ball bags were prized by the men of the mountains and proudly displayed when they visited an Indian tribe to trade and on special occasions such as the annual rendezvous.

CHEYENNE WAR CLUB

Make no mistake, the stone-headed war club, although primitive, was a deadly weapon and served the Plains Indians well. In trained hands it wracked havoc upon many an enemy.

The head of this versatile weapon was made from a stone, usually a granite one. The war clubs of some tribes had football-shaped heads 3" in diameter and up to 5" in length. These were pointed on both ends. They weighed as much as ten pounds and were attached to a 4 foot long hardwood handle. By today's standards, this would be referred to as the "magnum model."

The subject of this project is the Chey-enne version and is much smaller, lighter and easier to manage in combat.

Regardless of the size or appearance of the stone head, some shaping and chipping was required. A small amount of stone was carefully removed around the middle to aid in attaching it to the handle. Rawhide was used to secure the two components together.

The Plains Indian was a vain individual and decorated many of his possessions. Strips of fur, scalp locks, eagle feathers, etc. were used to personalize the war club to fit the desires of its owner.

Materials Needed

1   Properly shaped stone
1   3/4" x 16" hard wood limb
1   2" x 6" strip of raw hide
1   18" length of sinew
    Various items for decoration

Finding a correctly shaped stone may be the most difficult part of this project. If the craftsperson lives in the vicinity of a mountain stream or river where rocks rounded through time by rushing water are found, this is an excellent place to locate a good stone. If this is impossible, try professional landscapers; they often use this type of material in their work. As this project will probably not be used as a weapon, the type or hardness of the stone chosen is of no consequence (see *Figure 8-1*).

Chipping the stone is difficult work and there is always a chance the stone will break in the wrong place making the craftsperson start all over again. Spend more time in selecting the proper stone and

General Shape of Stone

AREA WHERE STONE
HEAD IS ATTACHED
TO HANDLE

Figure 8-1

as little time chipping as possible.

CUT TO LENGTH AND SAND
SMOOTH ROUND OFF BUTT
OF HANDLE AND DRILL
1/4" HOLE FOR LEATHER
THONG

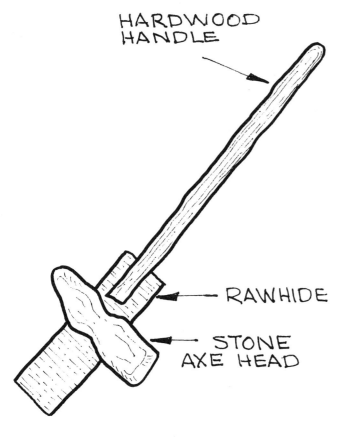

Figure 8-2

Select a 20" piece of hardwood for the handle; an oak, bois d'arc, hickory or walnut limb is preferred.

Strip all of the skin and bark from the limb and set this aside for a few weeks to dry. When it is sufficiently cured, cut the limb to about 16", sand all rough areas on

HARDWOOD HANDLE

RAWHIDE

STONE AXE HEAD

Figure 8-3

the handle shaft and round the butt end as shown in *Figure 8-2*.

Since rawhide is all that holds the stone to the handle, a good quality, heavy material is strongly suggested. Rawhide made from deer skin is much too light and will not do the job properly. With this project, rawhide made from a calf or steer hide is a better choice. Although the weapon will probably merely hang on a wall or be used at re-enactments, friends are sure to test the strength of the club and lightweight material may break.

Figure 8-4

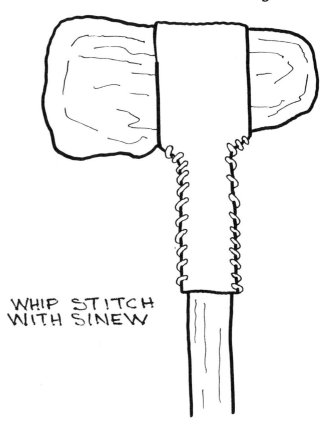

WHIP STITCH
WITH SINEW

Soak the rawhide until it becomes soft and pliable. Assemble the club (*Figure 8-3*). Fold the rawhide over the stone and use the awl to make stitch holes in the rawhide along both sides of the handle (*Figure 8-4*). Use a good harness needle threaded with sinew ("imitation sinew" available at craft stores will work) for this operation. Keep the rawhide moist during this procedure. Pull the material as tight around the head and handle as possible while stitching and take as much slack out of the rawhide as possible during stretching.

Remember, rawhide shrinks while drying and if sewn properly, this bond has great strength.

Drill a hole in the butt end of the handle and insert a 16" long piece of leather thong. Cut and tie the strip at a length so that the hand will slip easily in and out of the loop as shown in *Figure 8-5*. The Cheyenne did not like to lose his horse or his war club; he tied himself to both.

The war club is now ready for decorating. Feel free to use whatever items you wish, but remember the purpose for this instrument. It was used in combat as a weapon. Decorations should not include cumbersome items which would inhibit the actions of the warrior. Nor should hawk bells or other noise-making devices be used. The warrior depended on stealth and surprise. He may have been quite vain with his decorations, but he was not, by any stretch of the imagination, stupid.

Figure 8-5

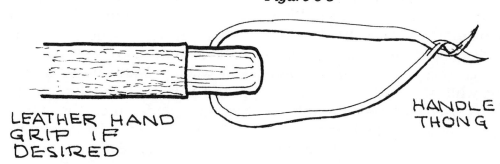

LEATHER HAND GRIP IF DESIRED

HANDLE THONG

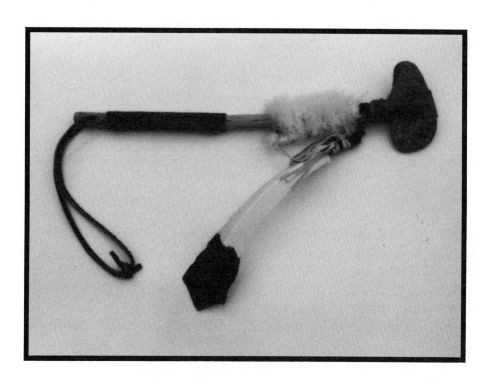

UTE BONE HANDLE KNIFE

The most common and cherished tool of the Native American was his knife. The blades of the early Indian knives were made of stone; jasper, chert or flint, and obsidian were sought after for this purpose. These natural materials made sharp cutting instruments but were extremely brittle and broke easily. When the white man brought iron and steel to the frontier, the Indians' knives became more durable. Blades were made from discarded wheel tires, barrel hoops and other pieces of scrap metal abandoned by the whites.

The Indians used various materials for handles; a piece of a large limb was sometimes used to make a nice knife handle as was an antler or leg bone of a deer or mountain goat. A comfortable fit to the hand and appearance were the two things looked for when the Indians made a knife.

When blades were made of stone they were sharpened by merely "knapping" off the dull edges. This act, of course, shortened the life of a good hunting knife. But when metal was adopted as the material of choice, a different method of sharpening had to be found and the Indians discovered blades became sharp by honing them on various stones. One of the most coveted natural materials used was a piece of petrified wood. Many outdoorsmen of today prefer this material for sharpening over everything offered on the market.

This project is a Ute cooking knife using a white-tailed deer foreleg bone as a handle. Bone is easy to work with, it is durable and strong when properly finished and makes a very attractive handle.

Materials Needed

1   White-tailed deer upper front leg bone
1   Knife blade
1   Quantity two part epoxy
1   Sand paper, steel wool and other
        finishing materials

Boil the upper leg bone of a white-tailed deer, from a freshly killed carcass, in water until all gristle and sinew slips easily from the bone. The bone will retain a great deal of heat for some time after it has been removed from the hot water, so be careful handling it during the cleaning process. An old pot holder works well to hold it while stripping off the residue. After cleaning the bone thoroughly, set it aside and allow it to dry completely.

Select a blade from an old kitchen

KNIFE BLADE MUST
HAVE TANG

Figure 9-1

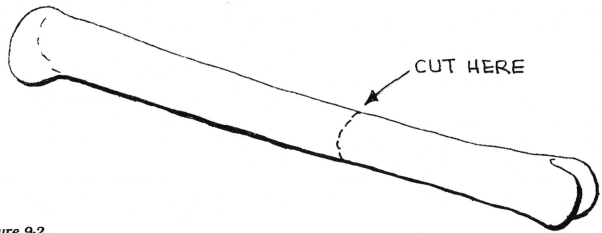

Figure 9-2

butcher knife or a new knife may be purchased at a local craft or hardware store. The blade needs a tang (see *Figure 9-1*) to mount it in the bone, so this eliminates being able to use an old pocket knife or other blade that has no tang.

When the bone has cooled, study it carefully. Note the joint on each end and select the end that is most pleasing to the eye; this will be the butt end of the knife handle. Hold the bone as if it were already a knife handle with the butt end against the heel of the hand. This will give the craftsperson the opportunity to get the "feel" of the handle and will also determine the length of the handle. Mark the bone where the cut is to be made and using a fine toothed saw, such as a jeweler's or coping saw, cut the bone perpendicular to the

length of the bone as shown above in *Figure 9-2*.

Figure 9-3

Look at the end of the section of the bone and notice the cavity running the entire length of the bone (*Figure 9-3*). This cavity is full of marrow which has to be cleaned out of the handle. A piece of wire works well

Figure 9-4

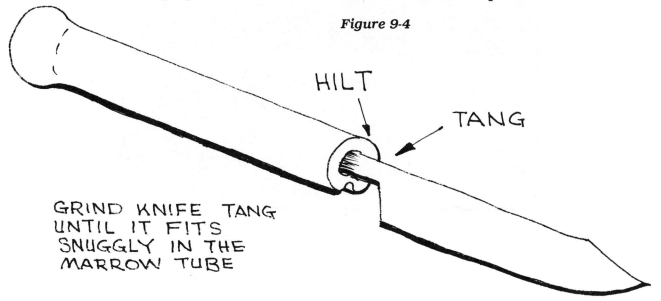

39

in this process. It is rather tedious and takes a bit of time to do it properly; flushing the marrow tube with warm water speeds the procedure. When satisfied that all of the marrow is removed, set the handle aside and allow it to dry completely.

The tang of the blade must fit into the marrow hole and a bit of grinding may be necessary to make this possible. Keep grinding and checking until the blade seats itself against the walls of the tube (see *Figure 9-4*).

Mix enough slow setting, two-part epoxy glue to completely fill the marrow tube. This will strengthen the handle and assure that the bond between the blade and the handle is secure. To protect the handle, it is a good idea to cover the entire handle with masking tape before placing the epoxy in the tube. Use a popsickle stick to insert the epoxy. This is tougher than it sounds as the epoxy will fill the hole quickly, but leave air pockets in the tube. Remove these air pockets by inserting a piece of wire from time to time as the epoxy is placed in the tube. Even with slow setting epoxy, work as quickly as possible.

When the tube is full, insert the tang of the blade into the handle until the rear of the blade rests against the bone. Slight adjustments must be made at this time to assure that the blade is straight with the handle. Carefully set the knife aside and do not touch it until the epoxy is completely cured (see the epoxy instructions for drying times).

Remove the masking tape and begin the finishing process. The sharp edges of the hilt end of the handle must be rounded slightly using a file and sandpaper. Ever finer and finer sandpaper is needed, ending with a No. 600 grit, to work this end to an ivory-like finish. Very fine steel wool is needed to polish the bone which will take on a beautiful soft patina finish.

Some craftspersons like to age their knife handles and this may be done by soaking the bone in a glass of stale coffee or tea. Be sure the entire handle is submerged in the liquid. It this is done, a light buffing with the fine steel wool enhances the appearance and gives the bone a beautiful luster.

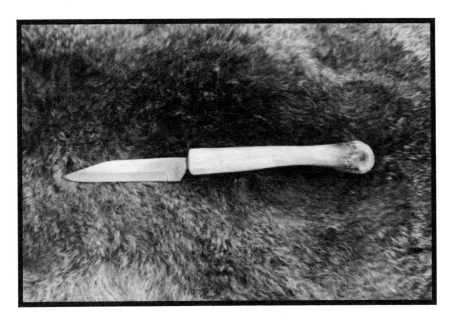

DISPLAYING A BEAVER PELT

Men left their families and homes to pursue the fortunes to be found in the Rocky Mountains. These riches were found in trapping beaver and trading with the Indians for the pelts they had trapped. Thus, a beaver pelt display project is significant to the craftsperson interested in the cultures of both the mountain man and the Indian. Trapping was a difficult and dangerous business and many mountain men lost their lives as they searched mountain streams for the elusive little critter. There are a great many books written on the subject for those who wish to pursue the subject.

All sorts of hides are displayed; deer, elk, steer, etc. and there are many ways to display such items. Some are used as rugs, some as throws over a chair or a divan, and some are nailed on a wall. Beaver pelts are difficult to find and expensive to buy, so, if the craftsperson is lucky enough to find one, it seems a bit of "special handling" should be considered in protecting and displaying the pelt. The following project will illustrate how to do this.

Materials Needed

1 Tanned beaver pelt or any hide the craftsperson wishes to display. The hair is not removed.
2 48" Choke cherry or willow limbs
2 30" Choke cherry or willow limbs
1 10' rawhide strip cut 1/8" wide
Decorations as desired - feathers, shells, felt, etc.

In constructing the display frame, choke cherry or willow branches are recommended, but any straight tree branches will work. Strip all leaves and bark from the branches and set aside for 3 or 4 weeks to dry and "cure".

When the branches are completely dry, cut two of them about 10" longer than the length of the pelt. Cut two more branches about 10" longer than the width of the pelt. Assemble the frame (see *Figure 10-1*) and bind the corners with rawhide as indicated. When complete, the inside of the frame should be approximately three to six inches larger than the pelt that will be used as

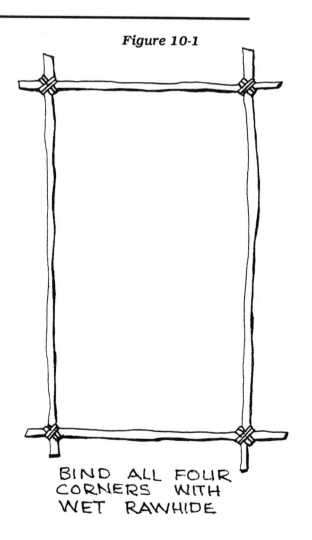

Figure 10-1

BIND ALL FOUR CORNERS WITH WET RAWHIDE

Figure 10-2

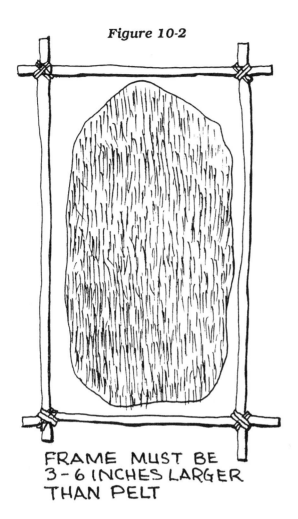

FRAME MUST BE
3-6 INCHES LARGER
THAN PELT

discussed in the Tanning Leather project.

When the pelt has dried, the craftsperson must punch 1/4" holes around the circumference of the pelt. A leather hole punch works well for this purpose. The spacing of these holes may vary, but should be no less than 3" apart and no further apart than 6".

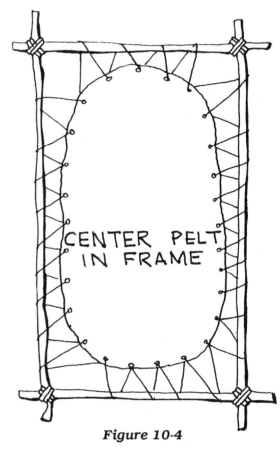

Figure 10-4

shown in *Figure 10-2*.

The beaver skin should be tanned (see the project on Tanning Leather in this book) and stretched to dry. Since the pelt is going to hang flat on the display rack, it is not necessary to "break" the leather. As the pelt dries it will become stiff which is fine for this purpose. If the craftsperson wishes, the leather can be softened by "breaking" as

Wet the rawhide strip and loosely lace the pelt onto the frame as shown in *Figure 10-3*. Do not attempt to pull all of the slack

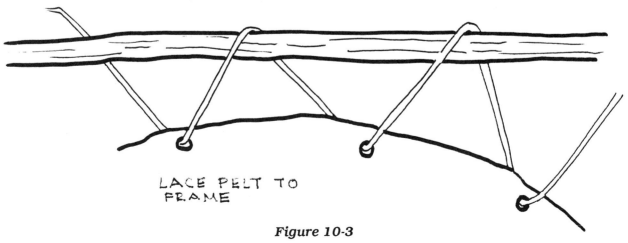

LACE PELT TO
FRAME

Figure 10-3

out of the rawhide strip during this process. When the lacing is completed, start at the beginning and slowly take up all of the slack, centering the pelt in the frame as much as possible. As the rawhide strip dries, it will shrink and hold the pelt rigidly in the frame as illustrated in *Figure 10-4*. Set the frame aside for a couple of days and allow the rawhide to dry and shrink.

The final step is brushing the hair on the pelt. Be sure and brush the hair down in the manner in which it naturally grew; an old hair brush works great for this step. If the hair is ruffled in places and does not lay flat, simply moisten it a little with fresh water and brush it dry.

Find a suitable wall on which to hang the trophy and enjoy this remembrance of the golden days of the Indians and the merry men of the mountains.

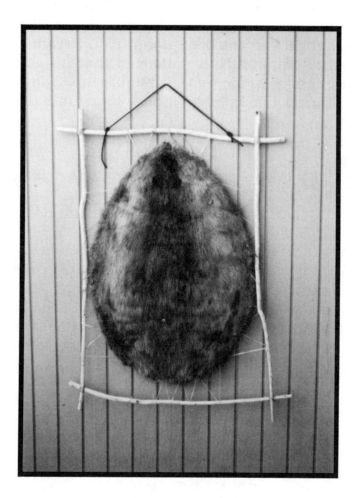

DREAM CATCHER

No one is sure about the origin of the Dream Catcher; it appears in many Native American cultures. The story, as told to the author by an old Pawnee gentleman, indicated that the original device was given to man by a willow tree and a spider. The spider told the man to hang it over his bed where all dreams from the spirit world have to pass. All dreams are caught in the web before they reach the sleeper. Bad dreams are held until dawn when they are destroyed by the rising sun's first rays. Good dreams circle the hoop and filter through the web, finally entering the mind of the sleeper. Each person must adorn his own Dream Catcher with personalized decorations. The Dream Catcher is an unusual item in that its charm is found in these personal embellishments. Beads are sometimes woven into the web itself.

Materials Needed

1   10 Ft. Imitation Sinew, rawhide or heavy string
1   24 Inch Green, fresh willow twig
    Feathers, beads, furs, etc. for decoration

Cut a straight, green willow branch about 24" long and 1/2" thick. It will taper to a smaller diameter but should be no smaller than 1/4" at the other end. Working very slowly from end to end, start bending it into a circle. Don't try to bend it into a hoop immediately; it will probably break. When the branch bends easily, form it into a circle (see *Pawnee Ceremonial Shield*). If a small hoop is desired, start with the smaller end of the branch; the smaller the diameter of the branch, the smaller the hoop.

Overlap the branch and remove a portion of each end about 1" from the ends of

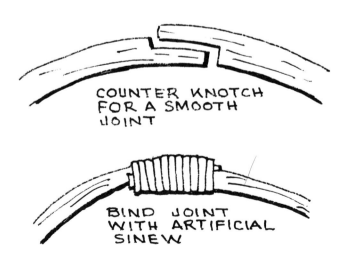

COUNTER KNOTCH
FOR A SMOOTH
JOINT

BIND JOINT
WITH ARTIFICIAL
SINEW

Figure 11-1

44

the hoop. Use a strip of wet rawhide or sinew to bind the two ends together by "whipping", as shown in *Figure 11-1*. Some craftpersons place fur on the hoop at the junction of the two ends; if this is desired, now is the time to sew it in place. Rabbit fur is excellent for this purpose (see *Figure 11-2*).

Figure 11-2

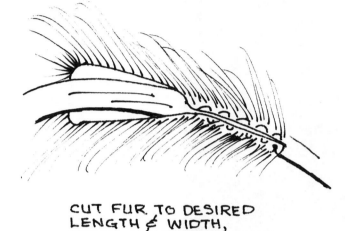

CUT FUR TO DESIRED LENGTH & WIDTH, STITCH AROUND HOOP

Figure 11-3

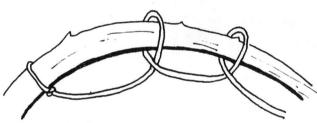

TIE STRING OR ARTIFICIAL SINEW TO HOOP PLACE EQUALLY SPACED HALF HITCH KNOTS AROUND HOOP

The material used for the web is now attached to the hoop. A good place to start is in the "whipped" junction of the branch. Tie the material to the hoop and use equally spaced, half hitch knots to fasten the web around the hoop, as illustrated in *Figure 11-3*. The more times the web material is attached to the hoop, the more intricate the web will be. Each loop must be pulled snug because the next loop pulls it towards the

center of the hoop giving the appearance of a spider web.

When the web material has been attached all the way around the hoop, proceed with a second pass around the hoop, using half hitch knots at the center of each of the first loops and pulling the new loops snug. Carry on in this manner, making new passes until the space inside the hoop is filled (see *Figure 11-4*). If desired, stop short of filling

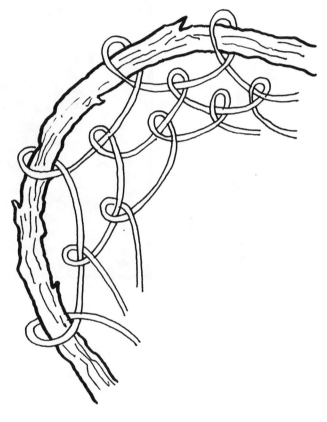

Figure 11-4

the whole interior and leave a hole or make space for some beadwork. Beads may also be strung on the web material during any pass. The end of the web material should be tied at its last contact point with a previous pass.

Now the hoop should be personalized to the desires of the builder. All manner of materials may be used for this purpose; beads, feathers and fluffs, deer dew claws, strips of fur, hawk or tinkle bells, even a bobcat's tail. These items may be hung from the hoop or, if not too heavy, from the webbing material itself.

COMANCHE HOOP DRUM

There were three kinds of Indian drums; the dance drum, the water drum, and the hoop drum. The dance drum was large, had a buffalo rawhide cover and was usually played by several men. The water drum, used by the Woodland Indians, was covered with rawhide and contained 3 to 4 inches of water in the bottom that changed the tone of the drum when the cover got wet. The hoop drum was smaller and more portable, making it ideal for use by most of the nomadic plains tribes - some had rawhide on both sides. The hoop was made from several different materials; some from thin strips of white cedar bound together to form a hoop and others simply from hollowing out a thin cross section of a small tree.

The drum was used in festive celebrations, as the people prepared for war, at dances for happy times and sad, and was one of the tools used by the medicine men during the healing ceremonies. Indian songs were always accompanied by the beating of a drum.

This project is for a Comanche ceremonial hoop drum.

Materials Needed

1   Cross section piece of a tree trunk
        2" thick and at least 14" in diameter
1   18" round piece of steer rawhide
1   1/2" x 18" chokecherry or willow branch
1   4" round piece of buckskin
1   1/2" x 36" strap of buckskin
1   1/4" x 48" piece of steer rawhide
    Wood chisels, mallets, hole punch
        paints and other decorating materials

Select a piece of a tree trunk for the body or hoop of the drum. It should be at least 14" in diameter; up to 22" is better if it can be found. The depth of the drum should not be more than 2 inches. On one side of the section, about 1 1/2" from the outside, draw a pencil line around the circumference of the slab (see *Figure 12-1*).

Using wood chisels, cut out the heart of the slab, leaving only the 1 1/2" outer rim for the body of the drum. Wood chisels are dangerous even in the hands of experts so use extreme caution when performing this process.

Round off the outer edge of one side of

Figure 12-1

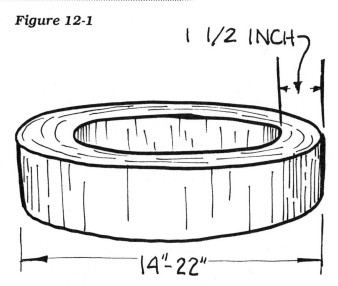

1 1/2 INCH

14"-22"

the hoop with a wood file and sand paper, as shown in *Figure 12-2*.

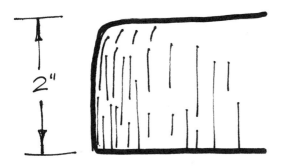

Figure 12-2

When finished, lay the hoop on a piece of steer rawhide and cut the drum head material as indicated in *Figure 12-3*. Using a hole punch, put an even number of holes, evenly spaced around the edge of the rawhide; the holes should be about 4 inches apart. Place the rawhide drum head and the 1/4" x 48" rawhide strip in water overnight to soften.

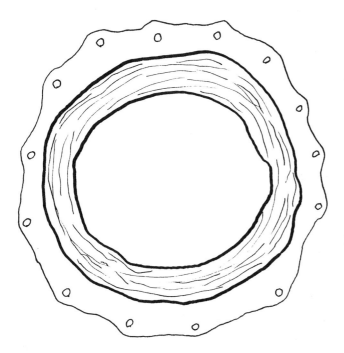

Figure 12-3

The next day, place the drum head rawhide on a work surface, rough side up, and center the hoop on the rawhide. Tie one end of the rawhide strip to one hole and work back and forth, as shown in *Figure 12-4*, until all the holes have been laced. Make the lacing very loose at first and be sure to keep the drum body centered on the head material, then slowly work around the drum, taking slack out a little at a time. It helps to keep the rawhide very moist during this process. As soon as all the slack has been removed from all the lacing, tie off the lacing at one of the holes and cut off the remainder. Set the drum aside for three or four days for the rawhide to completely dry.

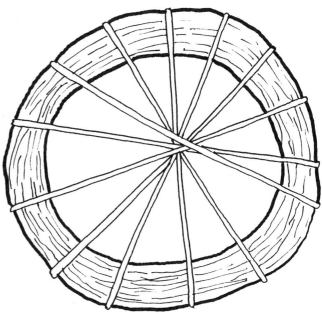

Figure 12-4

The drumstick or hard beater is made from a slender willow branch. Clean the branch of all bark and sprouts and set aside to cure. Sand the branch lightly to remove the chance of splinters and round both ends. Finally, wrap the beater end with cotton cloth or leather. Decorate with flat paint if desired and install a handle strip if desired (see *Figure 12-5*).

The drum head was usually decorated in some way; either to personalize the drum or to call out some outstanding event. Some painted their's with a spiritual symbol. The selection of design is left to the craftsperson but remember, Indians used natural elements to make their paint. All their paint dried to a flat finish. Don't ruin a good reproduction by painting the decoration with glossy paint.

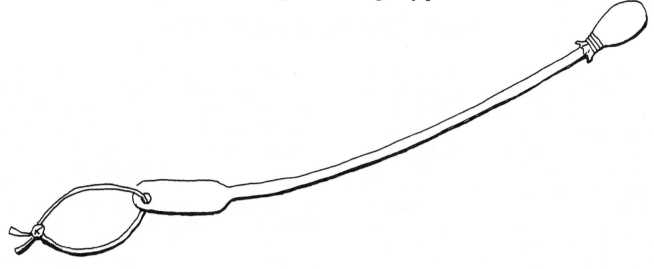

Figure 12-5

TRAPPER'S POSSIBLES BAG

Every beaver trapper carried a Possibles Bag; it could be compared to today's survival kit. His life depended on the materials he carried in this bag. It was his constant companion when he was in the mountains and especially while he trapped. The bag had to be strong - it received a lot of hard wear and abuse. It was not unusual for the bag to get wet as it was carried through beaver streams and in the rain and snow. Bags were usually made of smoked elk leather taken from the neck or the thickest part of the bull elk's hide.

There was no special size or shape. Each trapper fashioned his own bag or traded with the Indians for one of his liking. Some were made by Indian wives of the mountain men. The dimensions of each bag were dictated by what the individual wanted to carry. Trappers needed a lot of things to stay alive; extra rifle flints or percussion caps, gun oil, cleaning tools and rags for weapons, a fire starting flint, a flint striker, and dry tinder (a material used with flint to start a fire). Some carried fish hooks and line, maybe a spoon or cup and possibly a few spare trap parts. They carried only what they believed necessary; the unneeded was left in camp.

Materials Needed

1 8' artificial sinew
1 Shoulder strap
1 Antler button
5 Smoked elk leather:
      1 Piece, 10" x 10"
      1 Piece, 2" x 30"
      1 Piece, 10" x 16"
      1 Piece, 3" x 10"
      1 Piece, 1/4" x 60"
   Items for decorations such as beads

Using *Figure 13-1* as a pattern, cut three pieces of elk leather. The dimensions given are approximate, the craftsperson should construct a bag sized to meet their personal needs. Smoked leather is recommended; smoking of leather waterproofs and protects it from the elements (see *Making Leather*).

Use a sharp knife to cut the leather and be very careful during this step. A sharp knife cuts fingers the same way it cuts leather! Then using the awl, cautiously make the stitching holes indicated on the pattern. With a leather punch, make the holes on the ends of the gusset as indicated on the pattern; these holes will be needed when the shoulder strap is attached to the bag.

Thread a harness needle with about 2 1/2 feet of artificial sinew and use a whip stitch to sew the front piece of the bag to the gusset piece, as shown in *Figure 13-2*. Leave gusset flaps of about 2 or 3 inches at the bag opening, as they will fold over and help

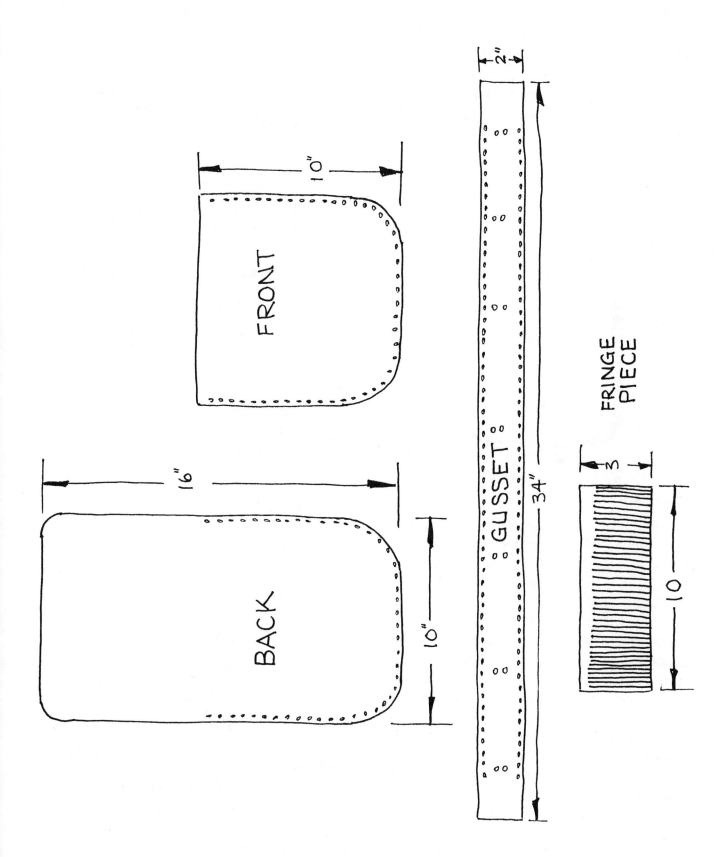

Figure 13-1

protect the contents of the bag from moisture. When the front has been firmly stitched, repeat the same process to attach the back of the bag to the gusset.

FLAPS FOLD IN
AND HELP PROTECT
CONTENTS OF BAG

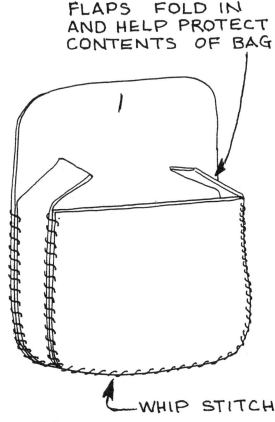

WHIP STITCH

Figure 13-2

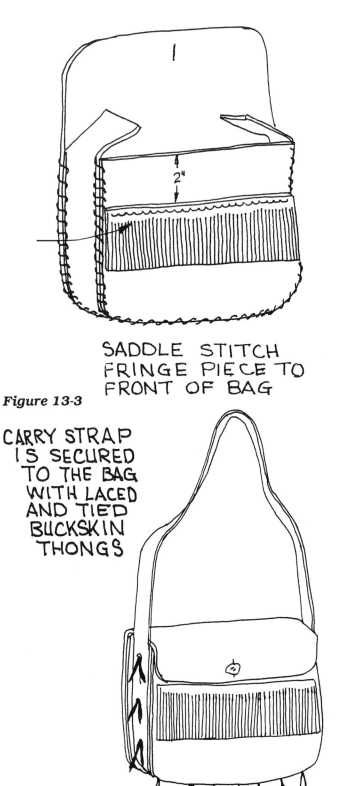

SADDLE STITCH
FRINGE PIECE TO
FRONT OF BAG

Figure 13-3

CARRY STRAP
IS SECURED
TO THE BAG
WITH LACED
AND TIED
BUCKSKIN
THONGS

Figure 13-4

Next, cut the fringe on the fringe decoration piece - the finer the fringe, the more attractive the bag will be. Saddle stitch the fringe piece to the front of the bag as shown in *Figure 13-3*.

Now, attach the shoulder strap. Punch holes in the strap to match the holes in the gusset. Cut the 1/4" strip into lengths of 6" and use these to attach the shoulder strap to the bag as indicated in *Figure 13-4*.

For decoration, bead a strip, 7 or 9 beads wide and 10" long. This beaded decoration not only personalizes the bag, but hides the area where the fringe piece is sewn on to the bag. Sew the beadwork to the upper portion of the fringe piece (*see Figure 13-5*).

Stuff the bag full of crumpled newspaper and fold the cover flap over the front of the bag. This makes the bag appear loaded.

Approximate the center of the flap and cut a button hole about 1" from the edge of the cover flap. Place a harness needle through the button hole and carefully press it through the front of the bag. This marks where the antler button should be attached. Attach the button to the front of the bag and enjoy the completed Possibles Bag of an 1800's mountain man.

STITCH BEADS TO TOP OF FRINGE PIECE, SIDES AND BOTTOM

Figure 13-5

UTE WARRIOR'S COUP STICK

To the young warrior, courage and bravery in battle were measures of greatness. Men were responsible for only two things; being good hunters to provide for their family and being fearless warriors to protect their family, band or tribe against all enemies. To kill an enemy was not considered a great feat; this could be done at a safe distance with a bow and arrow. True courage was measured by the coup - getting close enough to the enemy to touch him with the hand or a coup stick. Coup was counted differently by different tribes, but the first to strike was given the highest honor.

Many variations of coup sticks were used. Some examples are shown in *Figure* 14-1. A coup stick consisted of a slender stick; some were as short as 4' and others were 7' long. The stick was decorated with pieces of wool, feathers, horse hair and various furs. Decorative tack heads were sometimes used and often medicine items were attached to the head of the staff. As with most items used by the Indians, each was personalized to the wishes of the owner.

The coup stick discussed here features the "medicine" of a black tail deer. The owner of this stick claimed the spirit of the black tail deer to be his guardian and protector in combat. He honored the animal by placing an antler fork on the head of his coup stick.

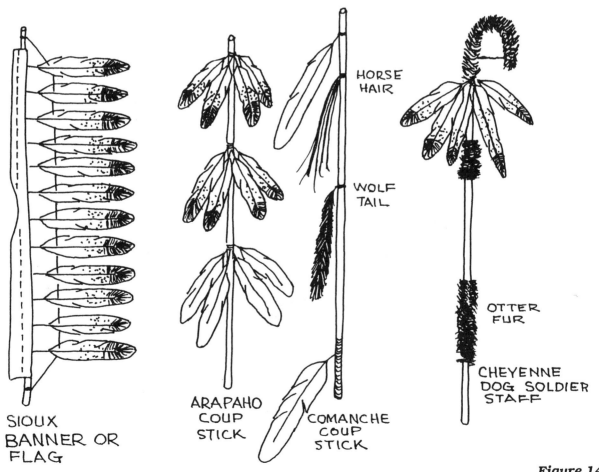

HORSE HAIR

WOLF TAIL

OTTER FUR

SIOUX BANNER OR FLAG

ARAPAHO COUP STICK

COMANCHE COUP STICK

CHEYENNE DOG SOLDIER STAFF

Figure 14-1

Red cedar, ash or oak work well for the staff. Remove all leaves, limbs and branches from the staff, strip off the bark and set it aside for a few weeks until the wood completely dries and cures.

Sand the staff thoroughly and remove all blemishes and burrs. Attach the antler fork to the staff, as shown in *Figure 14-2*.

Then prepare the feathers for addition to the staff. Glue and stitch two pieces of felt to each feather to form an attachment loop as indicated in *Figure 14-3*.

Use scissors to cut strips of rabbit fur about 1" wide. Cover the connecting point of the medicine antlers to the staff with fur. To do this, wind and glue the fur around the staff (*Figure 14-4*).

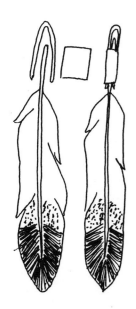

CUT ANTLER AND STAFF AS INDICATED JOIN WITH EPOXY

Figure 14-2

CUT A STRIP OF RABBIT FUR 1" WIDE WRAP AND GLUE TO STAFF

Figure 14-4

CUT A PIECE OF FELT 1/4" x 3" GLUE TO QUILL

CUT 2" PIECE OF FELT, WRAP AROUND QUILL AND STITCH UP ON BACK SIDE

USE LOOP AT END OF QUILL TO ATTACH FEATHER TO STAFF

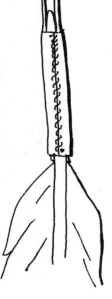

Figure 14-3

55

Next, wrap the piece of red wool cloth or felt around the staff and stitch the edges together as shown in *Figure 14-5*. Use a small hammer to pound brass-headed tacks into the staff (see *Figure 14-6*).

Feathers can now be added below the felt, and below that a leather hand grip if desired. The hand grip can be made by winding

Figure 14-5

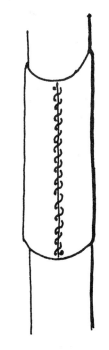

WHIP STITCH FELT
OR LEATHER
HANDLE TO STAFF

Figure 14-6

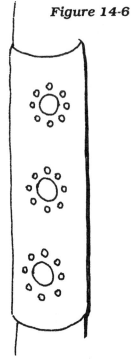

MANY DESIGNS
ARE POSSIBLE
WITH A VARIETY OF DIFFERENT
SIZE BRASS TACKS

strips of leather around the staff. Add other decorations as desired.

Protect the remaining uncovered wood with several coats of a 50-50 mixture of linseed oil and turpentine. Rubbing the finishing oil into the wood protects it from the elements and adds a luster to the wood. The Ute coup stick is now complete.

LAKOTA BONE NECKLACE

One of the most beautiful pieces of jewelry created by the Indians was the bone necklace. This piece was worn universally - by all tribes of the plains and by both men and women. Even when preparing for battle, as the warriors stripped down to their breech cloths and moccasins, many wore their bone necklaces. An Indian museum is not complete without several of these items on display.

Bones of various birds and animals were used to make these necklaces. Some were very fine bones, only 1/8" in diameter; others were often as large as 3/8 inch. The bones were cleaned thoroughly, inside and out, slightly rounded at the ends and laced on sinew with round beads and leather spacers between the bones. The length of the bones varied but usually were 1 1/2" to 2 inches. It is recommended the craftsperson purchase imitation bone beads for this project. There are many on the market and they certainly eliminate a lot of time and hard work; boiling and cleaning bones is a time consuming, messy job. The finished necklace made of plastic bones is almost as beautiful as the real thing and lasts longer. Real bone beads (cleaned and shaped) may also be purchased, but they are heavier and more expensive.

Materials Needed

18   Imitation bone beads
32   Barrel beads
3   Strips of sinew, 36" long
7   Leather spacer strips

Seven strips of leather are needed for the spacer strips. These are about 3/8" wide and long enough to place three bone beads side by side with a little space between the bones (*Figure 15-1*). When satisfied with the appearance, cut the seven strips to the proper length and with a 1/16" hole punch, place three holes in each strip to correspond with the bone spacing.

Place one barrel bead on a length of sinew, followed by a leather strip (using one of the outside holes in the leather), then another barrel bead, as shown in *Figure 15-2*. Continue this same sequence until the first line of the necklace is complete. Lay it aside and proceed with the second piece of sinew and complete the second and the third lines of the necklace.

LEATHER SPACER STRIPS
SHOULD BE LONG ENOUGH
FOR THREE BONE BEADS
TO LAY SIDE BY SIDE
WITH A BIT OF SPACE
BETWEEN THEM

Figure 15-1

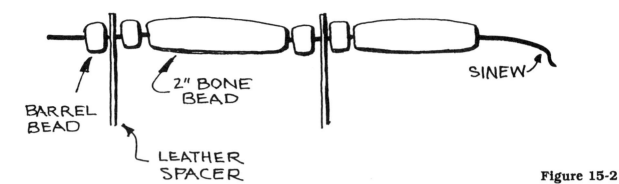

BARREL BEAD

2" BONE BEAD

LEATHER SPACER

SINEW

Figure 15-2

Center the beads on the 36" pieces of sinew and braid the remaining lengths of sinew together on each end. Use the braided ends to tie the necklace around the neck.

When the necklace is worn, tie it snugly around the neck. If tied too loosely, it sags and won't present the proper, dignified appearance.

If an old or antique appearance is desired, soak the bone beads in cold coffee or tea for a couple of days before the necklace is assembled. The longer the beads are left in the coffee, the darker and more "aged" in appearance they become.

APACHE PRAYER STICK

The sacred paddle-shaped prayer stick, known as "pahos" was decorated with god-like symbols and feathers. The sticks measured between seven and eight inches long and were used by the Apache, Navaho and Pueblo Indians in various religious rites and ceremonies. Small buckskin bags of cornmeal or pollen were often tied to the stick as an offering to appease or win the good will of their gods.

Many rules governed the making of a prayer stick. The painted design featured a particular god. Colors had to be exact and all pieces of materials left over from crafting a stick; pieces of wood, leather, even small pieces of feathers had to be reverently destroyed by fire.

Materials Needed

1 Piece of wood, 1/4" x 3" x 8"
   Paint and feathers for decoration

To make the prayer stick, study the pattern in *Figure 16-1* and draw the approximate shape on the piece of wood. Use a coping saw to cut out the handle and round the corners of the stick. Sand the stick smooth on both sides and edges, round the sharp edges very slightly.

Find a book on Kachina dolls in the local library and select a pleasing design; a few are offered in *Figure 16-2*. Sketch the design to scale on a piece of paper and when it looks right, transfer the drawing to the wood with a piece of carbon paper.

Paint the design using plastic model

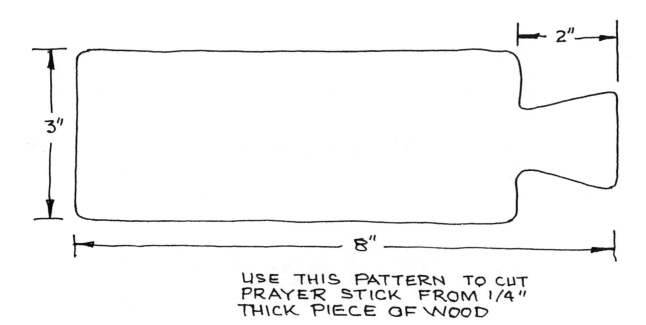

USE THIS PATTERN TO CUT
PRAYER STICK FROM 1/4"
THICK PIECE OF WOOD

Figure 16-1

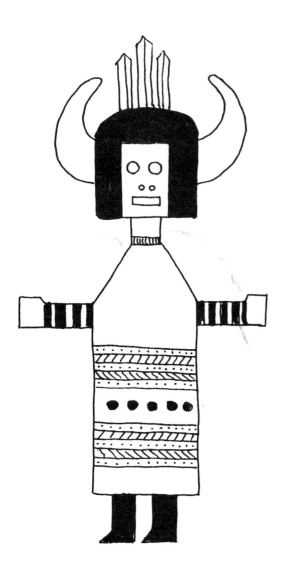
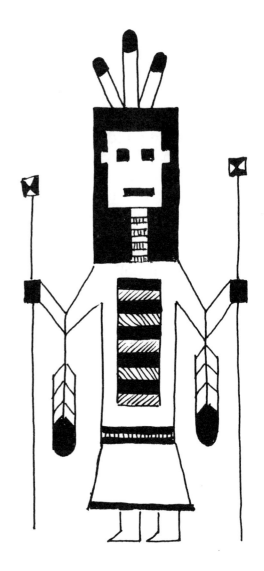

Figure 16-2

paints. Use the type that dries with a flat finish. When the paint is completely dry, rub the wood several times with a 50-50 mixture of linseed oil and turpentine. Allow the oil to dry between applications.

Attach decorations of feathers to the prayer stick and the project is complete.

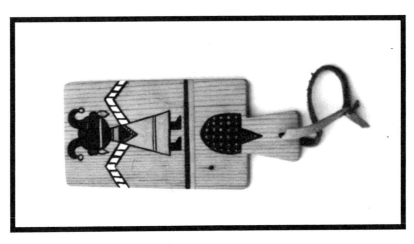

CROW DEER SKULL TOTEM

Indian cultures were filled with legends, myths and stories passed verbally from one generation to the next. Answers to things they could not understand were rationalized in a way that served them well. But there were many unanswerable questions in their lives and these things led them to be very superstitious.

Superstitions grow and control people in mysterious ways. It is almost impossible for people today to comprehend the manner in which the Indian was driven by his beliefs. Many tribes honored the grizzly bear and would neither hunt nor kill him. The buffalo or "wakan takan" was a revered god to many plains tribes and respected as such; the buffalo skull was used in many of their religious ceremonies.

Many of the mountain tribes held the deer in high esteem. Drawings of the deer are found painted on old buffalo and elk robes. The deer skull, complete with antlers, was displayed in tepees and used in many tribal rites and ceremonies.

A deer skull is easy to obtain and makes a beautiful wall hanging. The easiest way to get a deer head is to shoot one during deer season. The craftsperson who does not hunt should try contacting a local meat processing plant during hunting season.

Materials Needed

1   White Tail, Black Tail or Mule Deer head
1   Mounting board
1   18" piece of fine brass wire
    Stain and varnish

Great care should be exercised when removing the hide from the deer head. Skinning an animal requires a very sharp knife and that tool is dangerous if not used carefully and properly.

The skull has a great deal of flesh attached and there are two ways this can be removed. First, find a large, metal container to hold enough water to cover the entire skull. Place the container on a fire and let boil for several hours. As the meat cooks, it drops off the skull. All the flesh must be removed from the skull, including the brains located inside the skull. This is a long, time consuming and nasty job, so a second option is offered and highly recommended.

Place the skull in the freezer and wait for next summer, then find an ant den. Place the skull on top of the den and let nature take its course. It's a good idea to drive a couple of stakes in the ground and tie each antler to a stake using a good strong wire. There may be stray dogs, coyotes or other varmints around and if the skull is not secured to the ant den, it will certainly be missing very soon.

Check the skull every week or two; it normally takes a couple of months for the ants to do the job, but when they are finished, all fleshy residue will be gone - even the brain cavity will be clean. Wash the skull to rid it of any dirt and set it aside to dry.

A piece of white pine makes a satisfactory mounting board, but if the deep, rich grain of hard woods is desired, consider oak or ash. Select a shape of mounting board that seems pleasing (some possibilities are given in *Figure 17-1*) and cut the board to the dimensions given. Feel free to create a personalized design or shape, just remember to make the mounting board large enough to act as a good background for the skull.

Drill four 1/16" holes through the mounting board as indicated in *Figure 17-1*, then sand, stain and varnish the board. Three or four coats of varnish, with a good scuffing with fine steel wool between coats, will enhance the appearance of the wood-work.

Use fine brass wire to mount the skull to the board as shown in *Figure 17-2*. It's a good idea to wire the lower jaw closed when attaching the skull to the board. Drill a 3/8" hole in the back of the mounting board, about 1/2" deep. Pick a place to display the skull, drive a headless nail and use the 3/8" hole to hang the trophy.

A few skulls were painted with various designs, but most were left in their natural state. Some were simply decorated with a single eagle feather. The craftsperson may either decorate the skull or leave it in its natural state.

Congratulations, sit back and admire a magnificent wall hanging with a long Indian tradition.

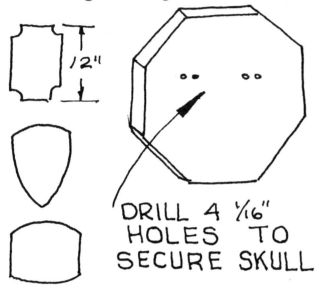

DRILL 4 1/16" HOLES TO SECURE SKULL

Figure 17-1

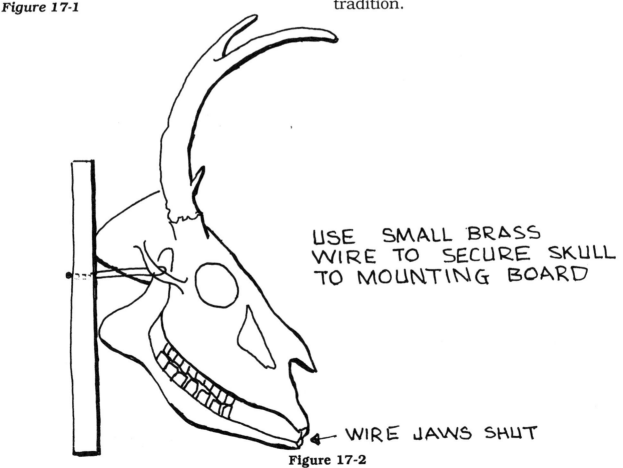

USE SMALL BRASS WIRE TO SECURE SKULL TO MOUNTING BOARD

WIRE JAWS SHUT

Figure 17-2

COMANCHE EAGLE FEATHER FAN

Almost all Plains Indians used the feather fan. Fans were carried by both men and women as they danced and they were used to keep cool and scatter flies and mosquitoes during the summer months. The fan was also an important tool of the shaman or medicine man; he used his medicine fan to brush illness or evil spirits away from or out of his patients.

Hawk, turkey and owl feathers were used, but a fan made from the wing or tail feathers of the eagle was a most prized possession. Fan handles were usually beaded and decorated with various items such as hawk bells, feather fluffs and pieces of fur.

Birds of prey are now classified as endangered species and protected by the federal government. Taking birds of prey, in any manner, is a federal offense and large fines make the use of such feathers too expensive to think about. It's even illegal to have such feathers in one's possession. So the craftsperson wishing to make a feather fan must rely on turkey, duck or goose feathers. Tail feathers from ducks and geese are too short to use, but their wing feathers make fine fans.

Materials Needed

6-8 Wing or tail turkey, duck or goose feathers
1 18" piece of fine brass wire
1 6" x 6" piece of buckskin
Decorative materials such as beads, hawk bells, tinkles, pieces of fur, etc.

Lay the feathers out on the work table as shown in *Figure 18-1*, with the longer feathers overlaying the shorter ones. When a pleasing array is achieved, make two pencil marks across all the feather quills. Starting with the longest feather, carefully use an awl to make a small hole in both sides of each feather's quill at both pencil marks. The sets of holes should line up across from each other as indicated in *Figure 18-2*.

Insert the brass wire through the two holes closest to the tip of the quill of the longest feather and twist the wire around itself as illustrated in *Figure 18-3*. Notice that the feather is turned so that the holes are on the top and bottom of the quill. Then take each feather and insert the wire through the holes as indicated in *Figure 18-4*. Bend the wire up and insert it through the upper holes of each quill on the top row. Come up through the bottom holes first on the bottom row of holes. When all the feathers are strung on the wire, carefully take the slack out and place the quills of the feathers closely together, as shown in *Figure 18-5*. Then wrap the wire around the first quill, twist the wire around itself and cut off the remnant.

Glue feather fluffs on the quills of the main feathers (see *Figure 18-6*) and finish the fan handle by covering the quills with buckskin (*Figure 18-7*). Beads should be stitched on the buckskin before it is sewn around the feathers. For details see the *Plains Indian Beadwork* project.

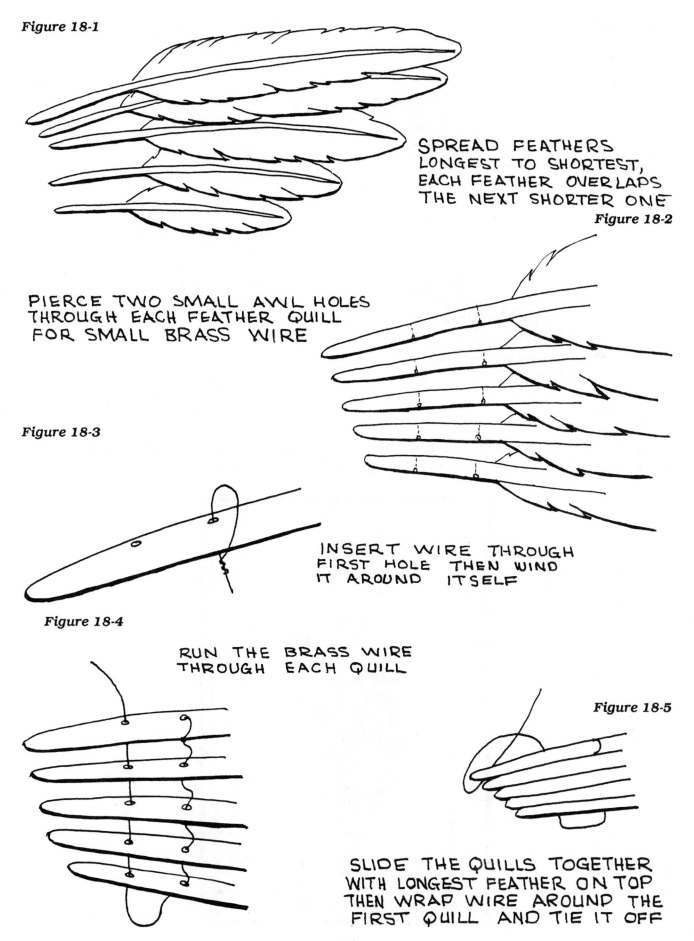

Figure 18-1

SPREAD FEATHERS
LONGEST TO SHORTEST,
EACH FEATHER OVERLAPS
THE NEXT SHORTER ONE

Figure 18-2

PIERCE TWO SMALL AWL HOLES
THROUGH EACH FEATHER QUILL
FOR SMALL BRASS WIRE

Figure 18-3

INSERT WIRE THROUGH
FIRST HOLE THEN WIND
IT AROUND ITSELF

Figure 18-4

RUN THE BRASS WIRE
THROUGH EACH QUILL

Figure 18-5

SLIDE THE QUILLS TOGETHER
WITH LONGEST FEATHER ON TOP
THEN WRAP WIRE AROUND THE
FIRST QUILL AND TIE IT OFF

Figure 18-6

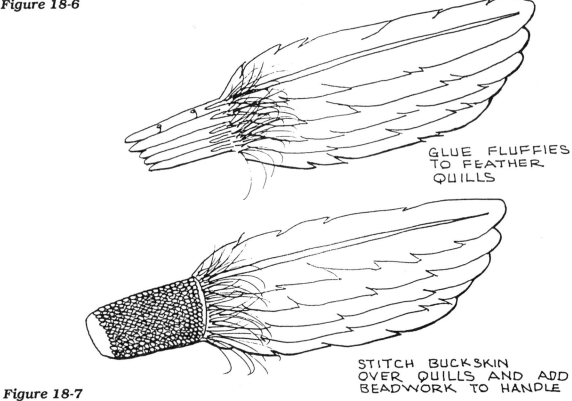

GLUE FLUFFIES
TO FEATHER
QUILLS

STITCH BUCKSKIN
OVER QUILLS AND ADD
BEADWORK TO HANDLE

Figure 18-7

Additional decorations, such as hawk bells, tinkles, etc., are now added to the fan.

Congratulations on completing a beautiful Plains Indian Feather Fan!

OJO DE DIOS

It's difficult to tell where the Ojo de Dios or Eye of God originated. There are those who believe it is a product of Mexico. Some say it was first created by the Incas in South America. Others believe it was first constructed by the Pueblos and used in their religious ceremonies. For several years Southwest Indians such as the Navahos and Apaches have crafted these beautiful wall hangings to sell to tourists. They are seen in Indian stores and trading posts in West Texas, Colorado, New Mexico and Arizona as well as other Southwestern states.

The Eye of God is a colorful explosion of dyed yarn. They are crafted in various sizes and shapes, and decorated with a wide assortment of feathers, tuffs of yarn, etc. With care and patience, the craftsperson can create a truly stunning piece of art.

Materials Needed

2   Strips of wood, 1/4" x 3/4" x 18"
    Skeins of various colored wool yarn
    Sinew or imitation sinew
    Decorative items such as feathers,
      strips of leather, beads, etc.

Notch the centers of the two strips of wood as shown in *Figure 19-1*. Make a cross of the two wooden pieces (see *Figure 19-2*) and bind the joint with sinew. Be sure this joint is exactly in the middle of the two strips and absolutely square; there should be four, 9" long arms on the cross. This completes the frame on which the design is placed. Take time with this step, the appearance of the finished project depends on a perfectly square frame.

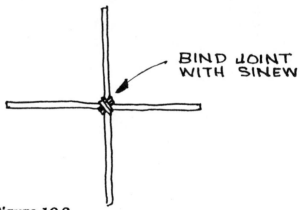

Figure 19-2

Take plenty of time to craft a design that is pleasing to the eye. Colors are also very important. Use extremes; light colors against dark when composing the design; this contrast makes a dramatic showing and enhances the appearance of the piece.

After the design and colors have been determined, cut about 10' of yarn of the first color to be placed on the frame. Wrap it into a ball; this will make it much easier to

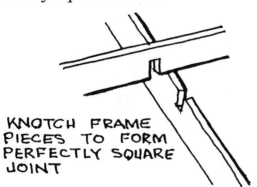

Figure 19-1

handle while weaving it on the frame. Tie one end to the center of the cross as illustrated in *Figure 19-3* and begin to interlace the yarn on the frame. Continue around the four arms of the frame until the desired area is covered.

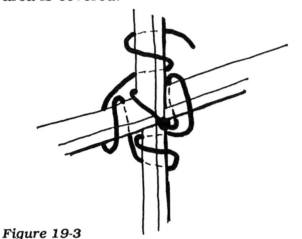

Figure 19-3

Cut the yarn and tie on the next color, using a square knot; tie it so the knot will be on the back of the frame and not be seen when viewed from the front. Continue this operation, changing colors as desired until the frame is completely covered. When completed, tie the yarn off with a knot and secure it with a small spot of glue on the back of the frame.

A loop is needed on the end of one arm to hang the piece on a wall. The other three arms may be decorated as desired with feathers, bob cat or raccoon tails, beads, fluff balls, etc.

The Eye of God can be constructed using any combination of colors or thickness of yarn or string. Figure 19-4 shows a few variations of frames shapes and construction. The only limitation in creating this magnificent reproduction of Indian art is the imagination of the creator.

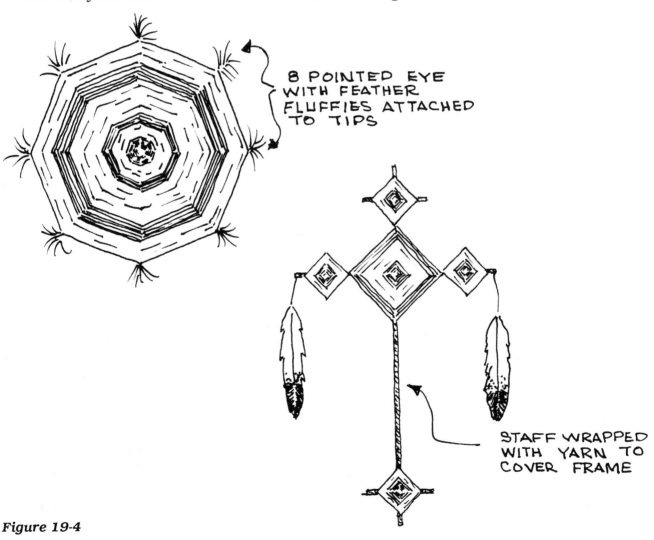

8 POINTED EYE WITH FEATHER FLUFFIES ATTACHED TO TIPS

STAFF WRAPPED WITH YARN TO COVER FRAME

Figure 19-4

PAWNEE CEREMONIAL SHIELD

A war shield was a brave's most valuable possession - it protected him in battle and was the source of his "medicine" or spirit power. The thickest rawhide from the buffalo's shoulder was used to make the war shield. When properly constructed, it protected the owner from spears and arrows, and caused musket balls to ricochet harmlessly away. The shield was painted with the warrior's "medicine" symbols and assured his success in battle.

The Plains Indians fought most of their battles from horse back, therefore an average diameter for the shield was about 18 inches. The war shield was used only for fighting and when not in use, it hung over the owner's bed or on a tripod in front of his tepee. If the warrior was killed in battle, he took his medicine shield with him to the other side; after placing his body on the burial scaffold, his friends and relatives placed the shield on the deceased warrior's chest.

The ceremonial shield resembled the war shield but was for ornamentation only and therefore made with much lighter materials. Designs were very personal, spiritual in nature, and extremely powerful to the warrior. One must remember the American Indian was an extremely superstitious individual. When fighting to defend his family, clan or tribe, he fought with no regard for his personal safety. But a warrior would go on an offensive raid, such as a horse stealing foray, only if his "medicine" was strong. If he determined his "medicine" was weak, he stayed at home.

Materials Needed

1   60" willow limb
1   20" x 20" piece of cover material, rawhide, chamois or buckskin
1   15' strip of rawhide, 1/4" wide
    Decorative materials such as paint, feathers, cloth, pieces of fur, etc.

Strip all bark and branches from the willow limb and slowly bend it in one direction to form a circle. Don't rush this process, bend a little, then release the pressure and move on down the limb and bend again. Bending too much will break the limb and the craftsperson will have to start over. Take plenty of time in forming this outer frame.

When the two ends meet, notch them so that they fit smoothly together (see *Dream Catcher* project) and tie them together with imitation sinew and a whipping stitch as shown in *Figure 20-1;*). Set the hoop aside for a couple of weeks to dry and cure.

Spread the covering material flat on the work space and lay the hoop on the material as shown in *Figure 20-2*. Trim the material around the frame, leaving about 1 1/2" to 2" to wrap over the frame. Use a leather punch to make 1/4" holes around the cover material and lace the cover to the frame with the strip of wet rawhide as indicated in *Figure 20-3* . If rawhide is used for the

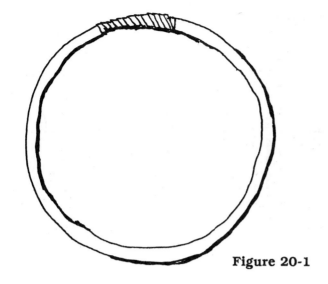

Figure 20-1

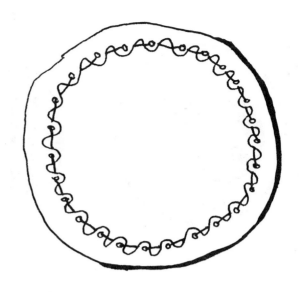

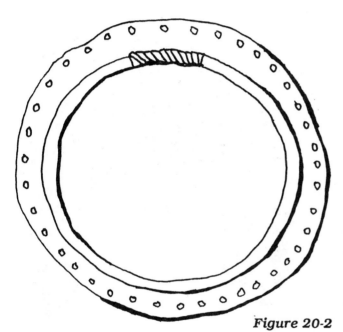

Figure 20-2

STRETCH THE COVER
MATERIAL TIGHTLY AND
EVENLY AROUND THE
HOOP - LACE SNUGGLY
WITH SINEW OR RAWHIDE

Figure 20-3

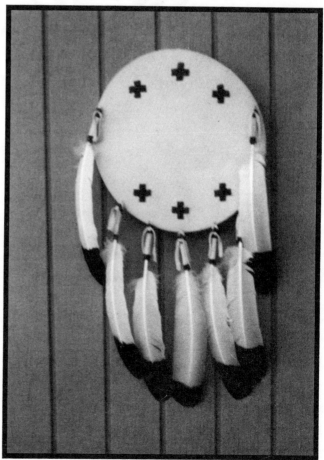

covering of the shield, it too must be soaked in water over night to soften it and make it pliable enough to bend around the frame.

Select the medicine design most pleasing to the eye and paint it on the cover with plastic model paints. Use the type that dries with a flat finish. *Figure 20-4* shows (next page) a few medicine designs found on ceremonial shields in Indian museums.

The ceremonial shield shown in the photograph is a replica of the Osage shield used on the Oklahoma state flag. The six crosses on the face of this replica were beaded on the shield cover.

Figure 20-4

MOUNTAIN MAN POWDER HORN

Two of the great concerns of the mountain man were his rifle and pistol. He spent hours cleaning these weapons; they were his only means of protection from marauding Indians and large animals such as mountain lions and grizzly bears. It was unusual for mountain lions to attack, but the "Grizz" needed no provocation to charge and kill.

When the white man first entered the mountains, he was welcomed by the Indian. It was not until much later that the tribes of the plains and mountains learned the white man's true desire was to destroy their way of life. During this period, the Indian discovered the advantages of the white man's weapons over lance, arrow and bow. He adopted the same concerns for keeping this new weapon clean and it's powder dry.

Dry powder was absolutely necessary for the old weapons to function properly. To assure this, the powder horn, long used by the white man, was adopted by the Indian.

Powder horns are exhibited today in various museums in the west; many decorated with elaborate scrimshaw designs. Mountain men were as vain as Indians about their personal items and some spent an entire winter etching designs on a new powder horn.

Buffalo horns were used in the west, but oxen horns worked well during the 1600's and 1700's when the white man lived in the East. After an animal was killed, the horn was sawed from the skull and boiled for several hours to allow the horn sheath to slip off the bone structure. The horn was then scraped, polished and finished. A well finished powder horn was cherished by both the mountain man and the Indian.

Materials Needed

1   Large steer horn, at least 12" to 14" long
1   Leather strap, 1/2" by 30"
1   Buckskin strap 1/4" by 8"
    Small pieces of wood and rawhide
    Brass-headed tacks

Many mail order houses offer cow horns. If the craftsperson lives near a beef processing plant, this is also an outlet to consider.

A raw horn is quite rough on the outside and requires a great deal of work. A rasp file is a good tool to start with as it will remove a great deal of material at a fairly fast rate. The best way to get started is to grasp the horn between the knees and begin filing. *Figure 21-1* shows a cross section view of a horn. Note the walls of the large end are much thinner than out toward the pointed end and that finally, the tip becomes completely solid.

Continue filing until the rough texture on the large end of the horn is completely removed. Care should be exercised during this process by feeling the inside and outside of the horn at the same time with the middle finger and thumb to estimate the thickness. If the crafter files through the horn it is useless and the project must be started again with another horn. As soon

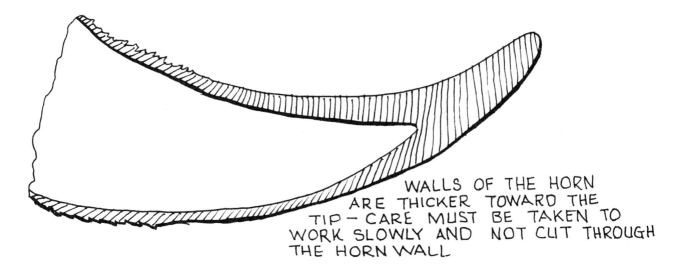

WALLS OF THE HORN ARE THICKER TOWARD THE TIP — CARE MUST BE TAKEN TO WORK SLOWLY AND NOT CUT THROUGH THE HORN WALL

Figure 21-1

as the horn is relatively smooth, carefully grasp a knife by the handle and the point and remove the file marks by scraping thin layers of the material. Watch the fingers, that blade is sharp!

Next start with sand paper and sand for several hours. Making a powder horn is an experience that takes a lot of time. Don't get in a hurry, stop and take a break whenever fatigue sets in. Use several grades of increasingly fine sand paper. End with 600 grit used with water. All that effort will be rewarded, as the horn becomes beautifully translucent.

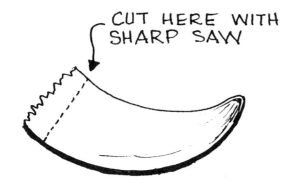

CUT HERE WITH SHARP SAW

Figure 21-2

The large end of the horn must be cut perpendicular to the general axis of the horn as illustrated in *Figure 21-2*. A jeweler's or model railroad saw works great.

This large hole is then filled with a solid wooden plug. Using the horn as a guide, draw around the horn on a block of wood; white pine is excellent for this job but any wood will do. If the craftsperson wants a textured wood, oak or walnut - although harder to work, gives a beautiful appearance to the finished horn. Follow the lines drawn and cut the large wooden filler plug. File the edges to approximate the shape of the inside of the horn as illustrated in *Figure 21-3*.

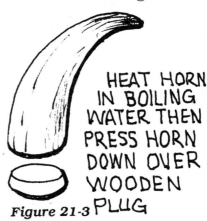

HEAT HORN IN BOILING WATER THEN PRESS HORN DOWN OVER WOODEN PLUG

Figure 21-3

When finished, set the plug aside and begin work on the small end of the horn.

Cut off the tip end of the horn to leave a stump about 3/4" across, as indicated in *Figure 21-4*. Drill a 1/8" hole into center of the tip end of the horn as shown in *Figure 21-5*. This hole acts as a guide for the finished powder hole that comes later. File, scrape and sand the tip end until it assumes the shape shown in *Figure 21-6*. Then use the 1/8" hole as a pilot hole for a 1/4" drill and drill the final powder hole, also shown in *Figure 21-6*.

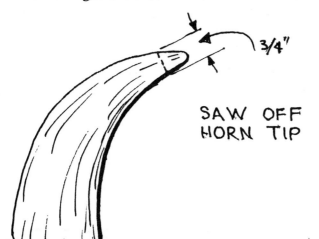

SAW OFF HORN TIP

3/4"

Figure 21-4

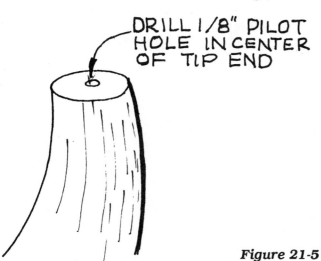

DRILL 1/8" PILOT HOLE IN CENTER OF TIP END

Figure 21-5

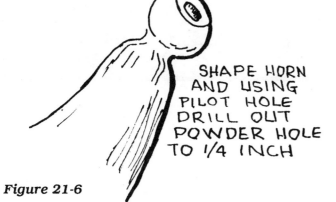

SHAPE HORN AND USING PILOT HOLE DRILL OUT POWDER HOLE TO 1/4 INCH

Figure 21-6

Carefully use a sharp pocket knife to carve a wooden powder plug as illustrated in *Figure 21-7*. This plug can be decorated by carving or using a wood burning tool.

The strip of buckskin is attached to the horn and the powder plug, as indicated in *Figure 21-8*.

CARVE AND DECORATE PLUG AS DESIRED

Figure 21-7

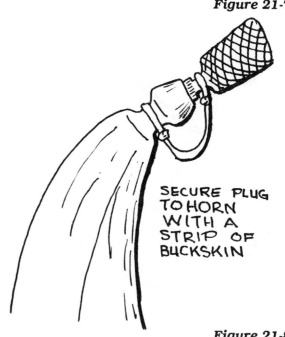

SECURE PLUG TO HORN WITH A STRIP OF BUCKSKIN

Figure 21-8

The large wooden plug is now inserted into the large, open end of the horn. As mentioned above, the shape of the plug must approximate the decreasing circumference of the inside of the horn. Do not attempt to force the plug into the horn; there is an easier way. Place about 3" of water in a sauce pan and put it on the stove. When it reaches a rolling boil, carefully submerge the large end of the horn in the water. Use a cook's mitten during this job and be careful, hot water causes serious burns. After a couple of minutes, the horn will soften and become pliable. Take the horn out of the hot water and place it on the wooden plug. When aligned properly, push down on the horn and the plug will slip into place. After the horn has cooled it will return to it's previous hard state. This joint may be wrapped with a piece of wet rawhide and decorated with brass headed tacks (see *Figure 21-9*).

Next, attach the shoulder strap to the horn. Use a brass tack on the large end (see *Figure 21-9*) and tie it around the groove in the small end of the horn (along side the powder plug strap). The powder horn is finished and ready for use.

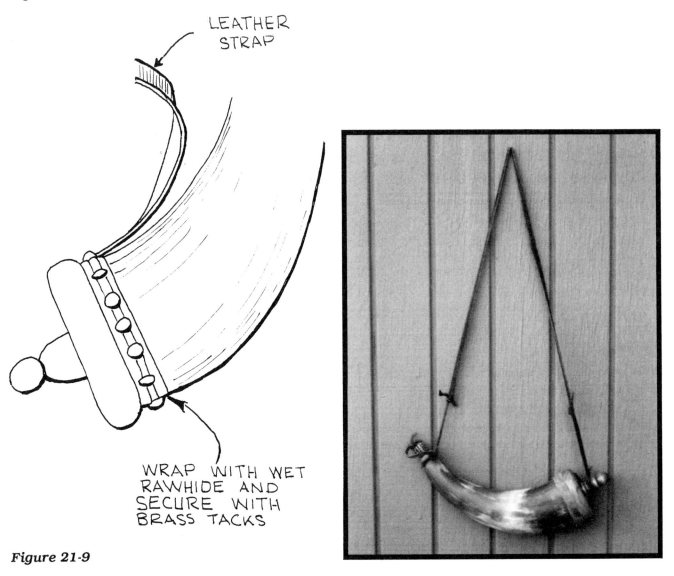

LEATHER STRAP

WRAP WITH WET RAWHIDE AND SECURE WITH BRASS TACKS

Figure 21-9

KIOWA ANTLER TOTEM

Antler totems were used in various religious ceremonies where the Indian showed reverence to the deer as a source of food and material for his clothing. Indians always prayed to the spirit of an animal before they released an arrow or fired a rifle. In this prayer, they asked the deer to forgive them for taking its life.

American Indians were the first conservationists, killing only what they needed. Nothing was wasted and every part of the animals killed was used. The deer hide was used for clothes, the bones were used for various tools and implements, the stomachs were used to carry water, and the intestines were used as storage tubes for pemmican - a mixture of ground meat, fat and berries which they prepared and ate in the winter when hunting was poor. Antlers were used to make various implements, as shown elsewhere in this book; even the hoofs and dew claws were used as decoration on other items.

To commemorate the close relationship they had with the deer, totems were sometimes constructed and displayed in Indian villages.

Materials Needed

1 Deer skull scalp with antlers
   Leather, feathers, beads, sea shells,
      paint and other items for decorations

Use a back saw to cut the antlers and a small portion of the skull from the head, as shown in *Figure 22-1*. It is important to clean all fleshy residue from the skull cap. This is easy to do by boiling it in water. The antlers and skull cap bone become quite hot during this process so be extremely careful; a cook's mitten works well to protect the hands from the heat and possible burns.

Mounting a small block of wood inside the skull cap with epoxy, as illustrated in *Figure 22-2*, makes it easier to hang the totem when it is completed. Paint the antlers with flat-finish, plastic model enamels; ring-like designs are attractive but lines running from the tip of the antler to the corolla are equally handsome. Indians used basic colors in their decorations and each color had special significance as

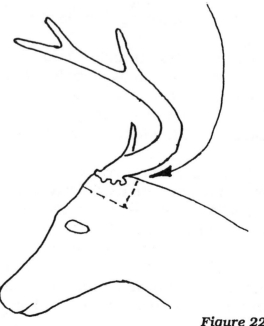

USE A SHARP BACKSAW TO CUT SKULL AT THESE APPROXIMATE LOCATIONS

Figure 22-1

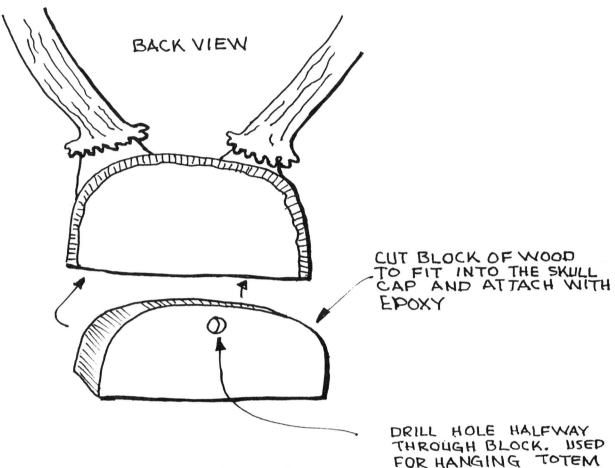

BACK VIEW

CUT BLOCK OF WOOD TO FIT INTO THE SKULL CAP AND ATTACH WITH EPOXY

DRILL HOLE HALFWAY THROUGH BLOCK. USED FOR HANGING TOTEM

Figure 22-2

indicated below:

Red	North, the people, life
Yellow	East, rising sun, knowledge, maturity
White	South, age, wisdom, spirits of those gone on
Black	West, thunderclouds, change, strength, victory in battle
Green	Earth Mother, growth, development
Blue	Grandfather Sky, the heavens

Now the totem is ready for decoration. Various items were used for this purpose; seashells, beads, deer hoofs and dew claws, feathers and empty rifle shell cases. These items represented an individual's particular beliefs and spiritual feelings toward the deer and may have represented personal hunting experiences the owner of the totem wanted to express to others in his clan and tribe.

The antler totem makes a colorful wall hanging and has a great deal of religious and spiritual significance.

LAKOTA PEACE PIPE

Possibly no other item represents the American Indian as much as the Indian pipe or calumet; it was a very significant and sacred part of Indian culture and religion. The pipe was used by most Indian tribes and was considered to be full of good medicine and strong with spirit power.

Smoking the pipe was a symbol of friendship and peace, so before any important conversation could take place or decision could be made, the pipe was smoked. The host or "head man" was responsible for beginning the ceremony. The pipe was loaded with "kinni-kinnick", an Indian mixture that included little if any tobacco, but rather a blend of leaves from trees, herbs, chips of roots and bark. The pipe was lighted with an ember from the fire and the ceremony began. The host was first to smoke; he first recognized the spirit of the sky by blowing the first puff upward. Spirit of the earth was next with a puff downward. Each of the four cardinal directions was saluted with puffs blown to the east, west, north and south. Then the pipe

was passed to the next smoker who performed the same ritual. After the completion of the pipe ceremony, the talk began and decisions were reached.

Pipe bowls were made of various materials. Some of the most sacred were made of red pipestone from a quarry in Minnesota. This stone was named Catlinite after the artist George Catlin who was the first white man to visit the quarry. This was a revered place to the Indians as they believed this stone represented living flesh and blood. Catlin was greatly honored by being allowed to visit this sacred place. Other pipe bowls were made of wood; even a large piece of elk antler was used by some tribes. *Figure 23-1* shows various bowl shapes.

Pipe stems were usually made from ash, sumac or witch hazel. The stem was from 18" to 24" long. *Figure 23-2* shows various shapes of pipe stems. Since the pipe was a religious item, it was decorated with various items. Many museums display several of these beautiful items. It is good to own one. It is good to make one and have it near.

Figure 23-1 (A)

79

Figure 23-1 (B)

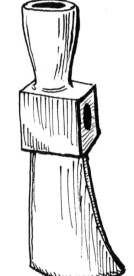

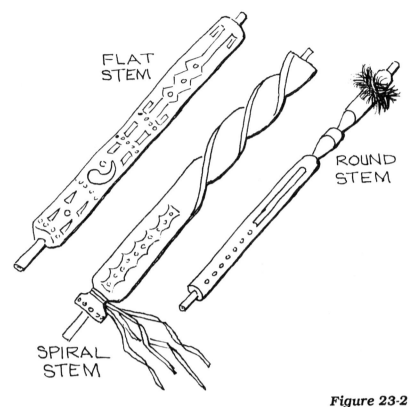

FLAT STEM

ROUND STEM

SPIRAL STEM

Figure 23-2

Materials Needed

1   Block of wood for pipe bowl
1   Piece of 3/4" x 2" x 24" wood (white pine works well)
    Decoration materials; fur, feathers, buckskin, etc.

Use the pattern in *Figure 23-3* to cut out the pipe bowl. The author used a large piece of oak root for the pipe shown in the photograph but any wood will work well. Carefully use a saw to cut the basic shape, then finish with a pocket knife, a wood file and lots of sandpaper. Do not hurry through the shaping process. Time spent in properly shaping and finishing the bowl makes a project to be admired for years. Before final sanding, drill a 3/4" tobacco hole as indicated in the pattern. Then drill a 1/2" hole to accept the pipe stem and connect the two holes with a 1/8" hole. Final sanding of the bowl should end with 400 grit sand paper.

The Indians burned the smoke hole through the stem by using hot wire. This is a long and potentially dangerous job, so another option is offered. Saw the pipe stem

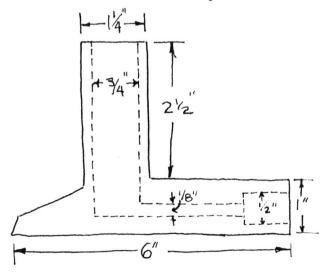

Figure 23-3

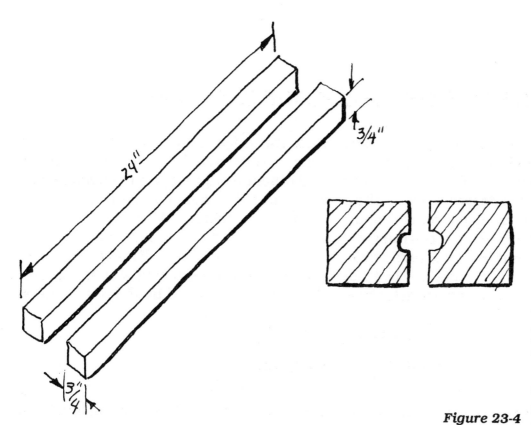

longer rounded section, goes in the mouth (see *Figure 23-2*). When the desired shape is reached, thoroughly sand the stem, using finer and finer grits of sandpaper, ending with 200 grit.

When both components are completed, epoxy the stem of the pipe into the bowl of the pipe.

The craftsperson should decorate the pipe stem in a unique, personal manner. A wood burning tool may be used to burn designs in the stem or it may be left plain. The entire pipe may also be stained and varnished. If this option is selected, do not varnish the pipe bowl and don't ruin the project with glossy varnish. Rubbing the pipe with linseed oil is recommended and gives a very nice patina finish. Use any other decorations such as tuffs or strips of rabbit fur, feathers, etc.

This project has a strong religious significance. It should be displayed in a prominent place. And remember, smoking of this pipe is dangerous to your health. Admire this addition to Indian lore, don't smoke it!

Figure 23-4

wood down the center, as shown in *Figure 23-4* and carve a small ditch in both halves. Then glue the two pieces back together. Be sure this tube runs the complete length of the stem.

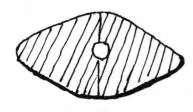

Figure 23-5

After the glue is completely dry, use a sharp pocket knife to shape the outside of the stem as illustrated in *Figure 23-5*. Note that both ends are smaller and round in shape; the shorter round end is inserted into the pipe bowl and the other,

KNOTS OF THE MOUNTAIN MAN

Rope was an important material used by trappers while searching mountain streams for the illusive beaver. When two things needed to be bound together for a short time, mountain men used rope. Some mountain men owned hemp ropes but most were made of thin braided strips of rawhide. These rawhide ropes were obtained by trading with the Indians, who were master rope makers. A few of the ways trappers used rope were to hobble horses or to tie pelts and other belongings to a pack horse; often a buffalo robe was tied to a tree to make a temporary shelter. Most mountain men knew and used only a few knots, but they served their purpose well and are ones that everyone should know how to tie. Most of these knots are used by today's hunters.

Materials Needed

1   10' piece of 1/4" cotton rope

All that's needed to learn the twelve basic knots shown in this project are a piece of cotton rope and some time to practice. Study the illustrations and practice each knot until it is mastered. Then try to tie the knots blind folded; often a trapper had to work at night without the benefit of any light. When this skill becomes "second nature" the student is a real outdoorsman! The knots in *Figures 24-1 to 24-6* were (and still can be) used to tie a horse, hang a carcass for dressing, or to tie up a buffalo robe for an overnight shelter. Bowstring or hondo knots (*Figure 24-7*) were used on lariats to catch wild horses. The hobble was common to both the trapper and Indian and was used to secure their horses yet allow them enough freedom to move about and graze - the large loops went around each front foot of the horse (*Figure 24-8*). *Figure 24-9* shows the bowline, which is easy to tie and untie; it will not slip or work itself loose. Indian halter knots were used to lead horses into camp from the herd; the large loop goes around the horse's neck (*Figure 24-10*). Sack knots were used to secure the tops of bags of flour or salt (*Figure 24-11*). The slingstone hitch was used to move large rocks and logs when building log cabins (*Figure 24-12*).

Half Hitch

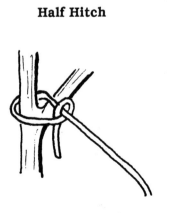

Figure 24-1

Slippery Hitch

Figure 24-2

Slipped Half Hitch

Figure 24-3

Two Half Hitches

Figure 24-4

Figure 24-5

Bluntline Hitch

Figure 24-6

Cow Hitch

Figure 24-7

Bowstring or Hondo Knot

Figure 24-8

Hobble

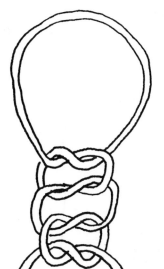

Figure 24-9

Bowline

Figure 24-10
Indian Halter

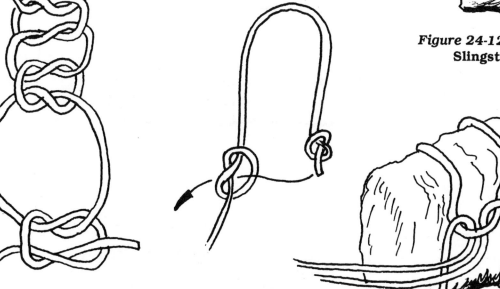

Figure 24-11

Sack Knot

Figure 24-12
Slingstone Hitch

TRAPPER'S KNIFE SHEATH

Every trapper carried at least one knife and many carried several; each had a special purpose. There were knives for self defense, knives for skinning game animals, and knives for cutting up a carcass. A special knife was used to trim gun patches when loading a rifle; this knife was used for nothing else.

The sheath served two purposes; it allowed a trapper to carry the knives safely and it protected the sharp blade edges. Every knife needed a sheath, even those carried in a "possibles" bag.

Since a sheath received a lot of hard use and abuse, it was not highly decorated with breakable beads or sea shells. But metal tacks or rivets were sometimes added to give it a little "personality".

Materials Needed

1	Piece of oiled leather
1	36" length of sinew
8-10	Brass-headed tacks for decoration

This project is easy to make in an evening. It's a lot of fun to put together and provides an ideal way to carry a hunting knife.

Lay the knife requiring a sheath on a piece of wrapping paper and trace around the knife blade and handle, then flop the knife over and trace around the blade as shown in *Figure 25-1*.

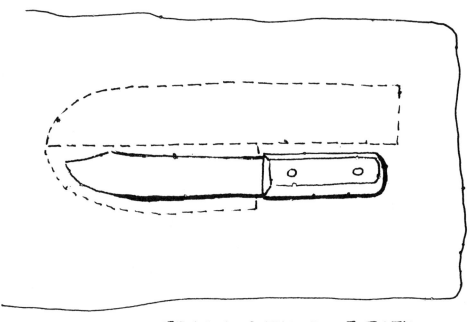

TRACE OUTLINE OF BOTH SIDES OF KNIFE ON HEAVY WRAPPING PAPER

Figure 25-1

Use this as the basis for a sheath pattern, such as the one shown in Figure 25-2; the portion behind the handle serves as a belt loop piece. Cut the leather to shape, using the pattern created for this sheath.

Fold the leather on the dotted line indicated in *Figure 25-2* and use an awl to make holes along the outer edge of the sheath. These holes should be punched in both pieces of leather at the same time as they must match up when the stitching begins. Use care with that awl, it's a sharp instrument and can make a nasty puncture wound! Use sinew and the whip stitch to sew the sides of the sheath together (see *Figure 25-3*).

Figure 25-3

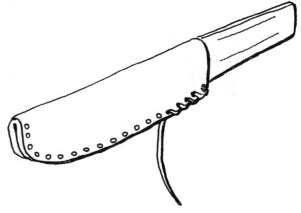

AFTER SETTING AWL HOLES FINISH THE SHEATH WITH WHIP STITCH. USE HARNESS NEEDLE AND SINEW

After the stitching is complete, cut two slots for the belt to pass through, as indicated on the pattern. To keep the knife from slipping out and getting lost, stitch a "keeper" to the top of the sheath, using an awl and sinew as shown in *Figure 25-4*. Use a leather punch to put 1/4" holes in the ends of the keeper strap. A short piece of buckskin serves perfectly as the tie. If a tie down thong is desired, punch a 1/4" hole in the tip of the sheath and string a 24" leather thong through the hole. Secure the thong with a cow hitch.

Rivets or brass tacks can now placed on the outside edge of the sheath. Any design is acceptable, and this decoration does enhance the appearance of the item. If

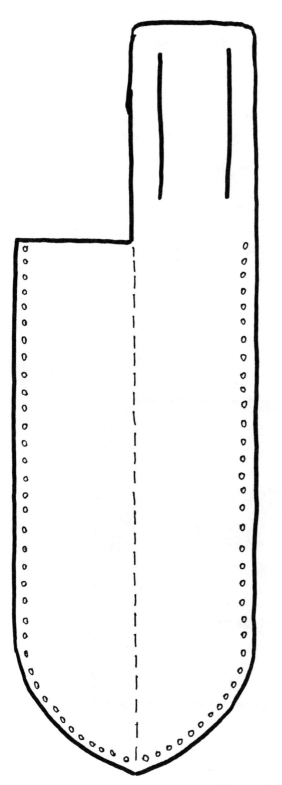

Figure 25-2

tacks are used, use a small hammer to pound the tacks through both sides of the sheath, cut them off with a pair of wire cutters leaving about 1/8" and bend this end over flush with the inside of the sheath.

Make sure these end pieces are "pushed" into the leather firmly so they won't snag on anything. The trapper's sheath is now complete.

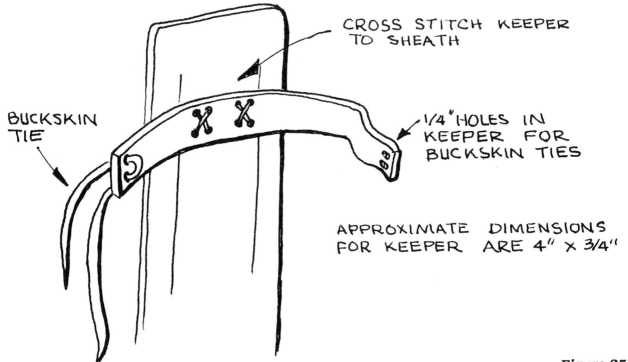

CROSS STITCH KEEPER TO SHEATH

BUCKSKIN TIE

1/4" HOLES IN KEEPER FOR BUCKSKIN TIES

APPROXIMATE DIMENSIONS FOR KEEPER ARE 4" × 3/4"

Figure 25-4

CROW PARFLECHE POUCH

The word *Parfleche* comes from the French and refers to a rawhide carrying case. Most of the Plains Indians made and used this type of container to carry and store their possessions. Some were trunk size (see *Figure 26-1*, lower right) and used to carry clothes, food, cooking utensils, etc.

The folded parfleche (*Figure 26-2*, upper left) was used to store pemmican (a special concoction made of ground buffalo meat and berries) and other small items.

The parfleches were made of rawhide and a big advantage of this material was its light weight. Most of the Plains Indians were nomads and constantly moved with the buffalo herds; therefore, heavy contain-

Figure 26-2

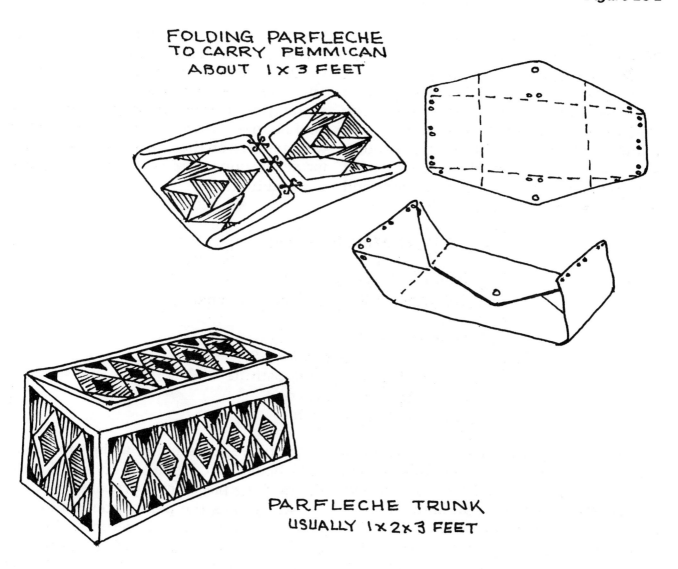

FOLDING PARFLECHE
TO CARRY PEMMICAN
ABOUT 1 X 3 FEET

PARFLECHE TRUNK
USUALLY 1 X 2 X 3 FEET

Figure 26-1

Figure 26-3

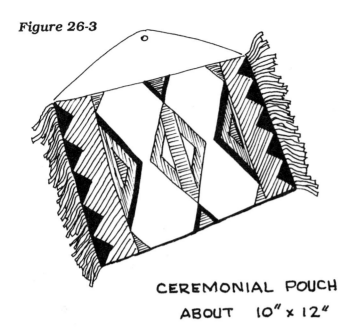

CEREMONIAL POUCH
ABOUT 10" x 12"

Figure 26-4

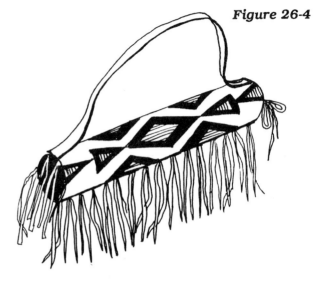

CYLINDRICAL CONTAINER

ers, such as the white man's wooden box, were of little use to them.

The size of parfleches was usually about 1' by 2', but some were up to 3 feet long and 18 inches wide. Pouches were made (*Figure 26-3*) in many sizes from 6" to 16" wide; many were small enough to fit in another small pouch. Cylindrical cases were used for crushable articles such as feathers and a warrior's headdress (see *Figure 26-4*).

Instructions for making a cylindrical case are covered in the next project.

These items were decorated by painting. The characteristic designs were simple geometric patterns dominated by large, bold shapes. There was no small detailed work painted on these articles. Colors used for decorations were red, blue, green, yellow and black.

Materials Needed

1   Piece rawhide 12" x 25"
1   10' piece of sinew or imitation sinew
1   Awl
1   Harness needle
2   Pieces of red trader's wool 3/4" x 10"
        Red felt is a good substitute
1   10" long strip of buckskin
    Paint and paint brush

Using the pattern for the ceremonial pouch (see *Figure 26-5*), carefully cut the rawhide to the dimensions noted. Scissors are recommended to cut the material when possible. Rawhide made from a white-tailed deer cuts easily with scissors. If a knife is used, great care must be taken in the cutting process; rawhide tends to be

slick on the surface and a slip of a sharp knife blade can cause a bad cut and destroy the rawhide piece being prepared.

Next comes the painted design for the pouch. Study several pictures, illustrations and photographs before starting to draw the paintings. The design used in this project comes from the Crow people. However, each tribe's decorations were special to them and were easily recognizable to the trained eye. The craftsperson should attempt to make a good reproduction of this pouch, including the design used.

After finding a design that pleases, use a straight edge, such as a ruler, with a pencil and paper and carefully reproduce the design on the paper. This drawing should be made to the full scale of the

Figure 26-5

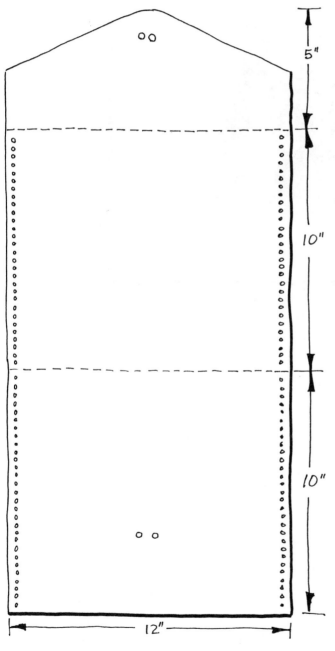

pouch. When the design is complete, use a sheet of carbon paper and transfer the design to the rawhide. Use a ruler to keep all of the lines straight.

Painting the design is exacting work and takes a great deal of patience to do a good job. Since this is a very important part of the pouch, take time and be as precise as possible with the painting; a small artist's brush (such as No. 0) is recommended. Both sides may be painted or just the front side and flap. Suitable paints to use are "earth paints," available from some craft stores or those available where plastic models are sold. Be sure and select the "flat" enamel paint. The Indians used paints made from various chemicals found in nature and this paint dried dull or flat. To use a gloss enamel on parfleche immediately lets everyone know that the craftsperson didn't know much about Indians.

When the paint is completely dry, punch four holes; two in the flap, and two in the front side of the pouch (*Figure 26-5*). These holes are for the buckskin thong that is used to tie the pouch shut. Using the edge of a workbench as a straight edge, fold the face of the pouch over to meet the back side. The folds are rounded, not squarely bent or creased. This provides a bit of expansion so

Figure 26-6

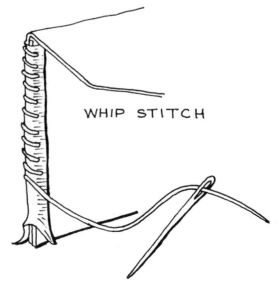

WHIP STITCH

various items will fit into the pouch.

The edges of the pouch are trimmed with red felt material and whip stitched with sinew, as shown in *Figure 26-6*. Use a block of soft wood to protect the point of the awl as these holes are made. A word of caution: The awl makes nasty stab wounds in the hands of the careless. Be Careful! Punch the awl holes and stitch the sides of the pouch using the whip stitch.

Thread the buckskin thong through the holes in the face of the pouch and tie a knot in the thong. The remainder of the thong is used as a latch to tie the pouch shut after it has been filled with items.

BLACKFOOT CEREMONIAL CASE

Cylindrical parfleche containers were used as medicine bundles and to carry or store items of a religious nature. They were used by most of the Plains Indians (for background information see *Crow Parfleche Pouch* project). The design on this reproduction is characteristic of the Blackfoot people. These containers were carefully painted, using paint made of natural elements. In addition to the bold painted design, the cylinder containers were also decorated with a great deal of fringe.

Materials Needed	
1	Piece of deer rawhide, 16" by 9"
2	Round pieces of rawhide, 2 1/2" in diam.
45	Strips of buckskin 16" to 18" long
1	24" piece of sinew or artificial sinew
1	24" by 1/2" buckskin strap
	Awl, paint and paint brush

Use *Figure 27-1* as a guide for the three pieces of rawhide needed for the project. Scissors are recommended to cut the rawhide. If a knife is used, be very careful. Rawhide can be very hard to cut with a knife and a slip can cause a serious cut. Holes are needed on three sides of the large piece about 1/4" apart and around one of the round pieces. Four holes are needed in the remaining side of the large rawhide piece, which will become the top of the cylinder. Matching holes in the second round piece, which will become the lid, are also needed. Carefully, use an awl to punch the holes as

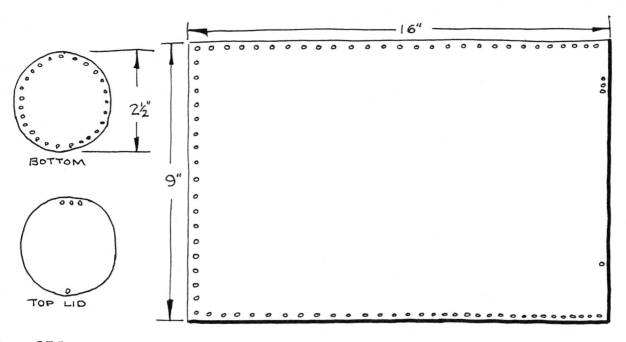

Figure 27-1

CHEYENNE   CROW   HIDATSA

Figure 27-2

indicated. Use a soft piece of wood to back up the rawhide when using the awl; this will protect the surface of the work table.

The next step in constructing this project is the selection of a good design. No small detail work is found on the parfleche - only bold, simple geometric designs were used. *Figure 27-2* offers some suggestions. Pick one that pleases the senses or design an original. Draw the design, full scale on a piece of paper. The design should fit on the large piece of rawhide with margins all around. Use a ruler to assure all edges are straight. When the design is satisfactory, transfer it to the rawhide with help from a piece of carbon paper. Use "flat" paints; red, yellow, blue, green and black to paint the design. The flat finish paints designed for plastic models work fine for this purpose. Do not use glossy enamels to paint the parfleche. Indians used paints made from natural elements and shining paint on parfleche is never seen.

After the paint dries, construction of the tube may begin. Using *Figure 27-3* as a guide, gently curl the flat piece of rawhide and begin to insert the buckskin strips.

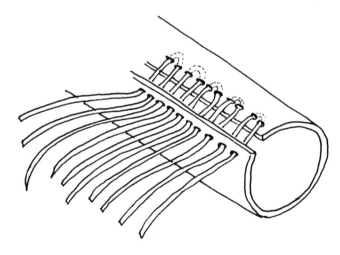

Figure 27-3

Don't attempt to pull these strips tight or tie them until all the strips are in place. As soon as all the strips are in place, start from one end and work all the slack out of each strip. After the slack is taken up, tie each strip with a square knot, as shown in *Figure 27-4*.

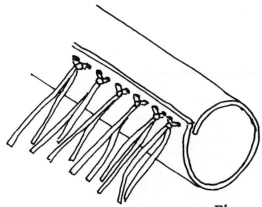

Figure 27-4

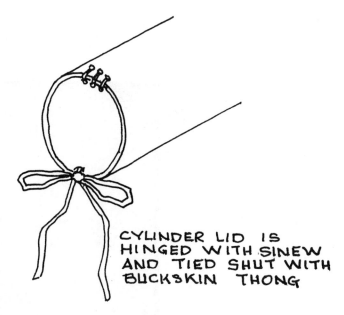

CYLINDER LID IS
HINGED WITH SINEW
AND TIED SHUT WITH
BUCKSKIN THONG

Figure 27-6

When this step is finished the tube is complete, including long, flowing fringe decoration. Now the bottom of the tube must be closed with the round piece of rawhide having awl-punched holes all around the edge. This is done in the same way as the tube. Insert all the strips, then take out all the slack and tie the fringe strips with square knots. Be sure to leave long decorative fringe (see *Figure 27-5*).

The last step is the hanging strap which is made from the 24" by 1/2" buckskin strap. Using sinew, attach the strap to the bottom and top ends of the container, punching holes where needed as illustrated in *Figure 27-7*. This strap was used to hang the cylindrical parfleche from a tepee pole or tripod.

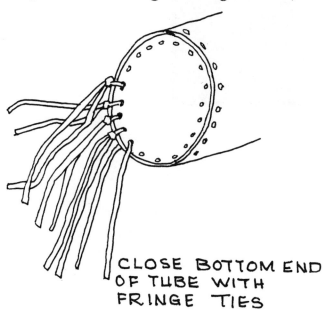

CLOSE BOTTOM END
OF TUBE WITH
FRINGE TIES

Figure 27-5

The other end of the case is covered with a movable lid. The lid is attached to the tube with sinew. Make a lace hinge, using the sets of three holes as shown in *Figure 27-6*, then thread a buckskin strap through the holes in the lid and the edge of the tube to tie the cover shut.

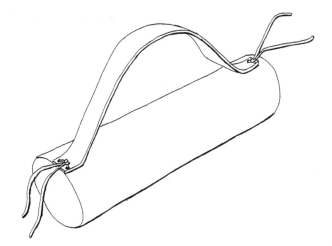

Figure 27-7

UTE PARFLECHE KNIFE SHEATH

In addition to using rawhide to make parfleche containers, the material was also used to make several other items. One such item was a knife sheath.

No Indian, man or woman, would ever be without their knife; it was always worn, even as they slept. Knives came in different sizes and shapes, depending on the task required, but all were carried in a leather or rawhide sheath. If rawhide was used, it offered an opportunity for a painted design. No Indian or mountain man would ever pass up an opportunity to "make a fancy" of any personal article.

The rawhide sheath is easy to construct in one evening and makes a dandy way to carry a hunting knife.

Materials Needed

1   Piece of steer rawhide
1   24" rawhide strip, 1/16" wide
    Plastic model paints, flat finish

Lay the rawhide on a suitable work surface. Place the knife on the material, as shown in *Figure 28-1* and draw the pattern or outline of the blade on the rawhide. Leave enough rawhide at the hilt end of the material to fold backwards for a belt loop. When satisfied with the shape, carefully cut the piece from the rawhide. Use many passes with the knife when cutting thick rawhide; it is nearly impossible to cut all the way through with the first pass. Use extreme care in this process, because knife cuts can be nasty.

This first piece forms the back portion of the sheath. Using it as a pattern, place it upside down on the rawhide and trace around it as indicated in *Figure 28-2*. Notice that the extra rawhide for the belt loop

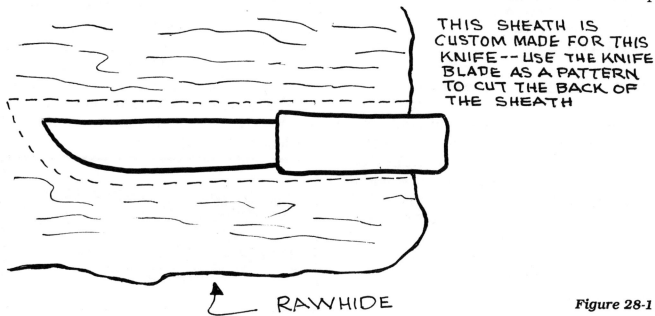

THIS SHEATH IS CUSTOM MADE FOR THIS KNIFE -- USE THE KNIFE BLADE AS A PATTERN TO CUT THE BACK OF THE SHEATH

RAWHIDE

Figure 28-1

is not included. Cut out this second piece, which will form the front of the sheath.

USE THE BACK OF THE SHEATH AS A PATTERN TO CUT THE FRONT

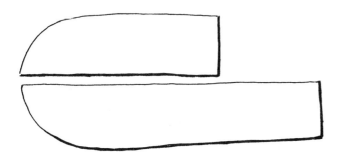

Figure 28-2

Place the two halves together and use a 1/16" hole punch to place holes around the outside edges of the material, as illustrated in *Figure 28-3*. Punch both pieces of rawhide at the same time to assure the holes will match up.

PUNCH 1/16" HOLES IN THE FRONT AND BACK OF THE SHEATH   *Figure 28-3*

Place the thin rawhide strip in hot water for a couple of hours or until it becomes very flexible. Hold the two halves in position and begin to whip stitch the sheath together with the rawhide strip as shown in *Figure 28-4*. Partway down the first edge, fold the belt loop over and punch a couple of holes in the end of it. Stitch the end of the belt loop to both edges of the sheath during the lacing process (see *Figure 28-5*). Set the sheath aside for a couple of hours and allow the lacing to dry and shrink.

USE THE WHIP STITCH TO SEW THE FRONT TO THE BACK OF THE SHEATH

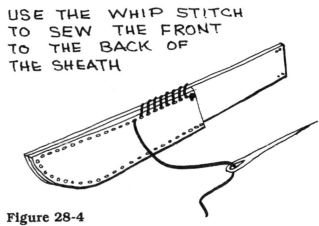

Figure 28-4

STITCH BELT LOOP TO BACK OF SHEATH

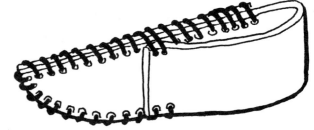

Figure 28-5

While waiting for the rawhide strip to dry, pencil several designs on a piece of scrap paper. Remember, parfleche designs were large and bold in nature, with no small intricate designs. The knife sheath isn't large so the design has to be relatively simple.

When satisfied with the design, draw it full scale and transfer it onto the face of the sheath using carbon paper. The best paints to use are those used to paint plastic models. The Indian made his paints from natural elements and they dried with a dull or flat finish. Use flat enamels when painting the design, glossy paint tells everyone the maker of the sheath knew little of parfleche painting.

PERSONAL TOTEM

Indian cultures used many totems in their personal lives and in various ceremonies. The totem represented an animal or natural object considered to be related by blood or spirit to a given individual. It was displayed to show special, personal symbols representing the totem's owner.

Some tribes painted their totem symbols on the outside of their tepees; a warrior always painted his totem on his war shield. Sometimes the totem was placed on a small piece of rawhide and hung on a tripod in front of the tepee; when used in this manner it acted as a name plate for the residence.

Materials Needed

2   Willow limbs, 18" long
2   Willow limbs, 12" long
1   Piece of rawhide, 10" x 16"
1   60" strip of rawhide, 1/4" wide
1   24" leather thong
      Paint, feathers, fur and any other
        items for decoration

Strip the bark, leaves and small branches from the willow limbs and set them aside for a couple of weeks to completely dry and cure.

Use the willow limbs to make a frame for the totem. Bind the four corners with strips of wet rawhide (see *Figure 29-1*). Place the rawhide on a work surface and lay the frame around it as shown in *Figure 29-2*. The

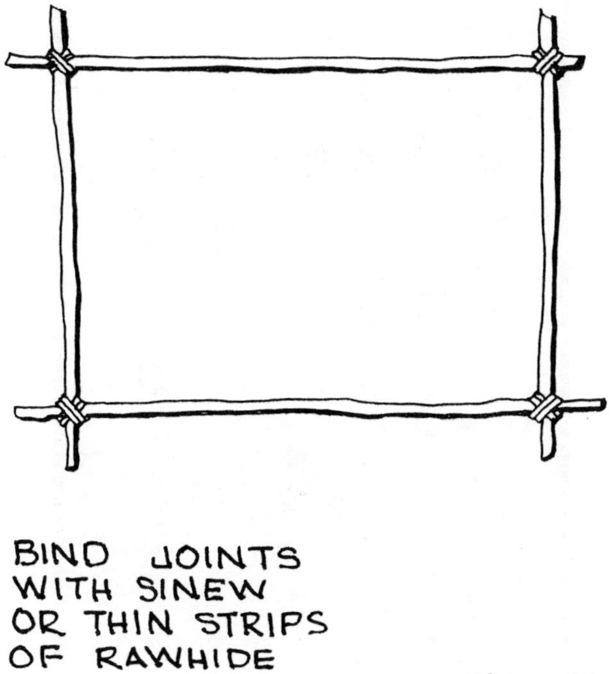

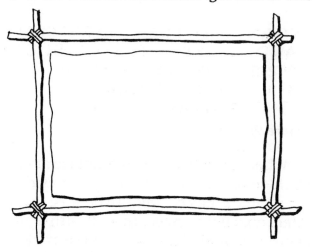

BIND JOINTS
WITH SINEW
OR THIN STRIPS
OF RAWHIDE

RAWHIDE PANEL
SHOULD BE ONE
INCH SMALLER
THAN FRAME
ALL THE WAY
AROUND

Figure 29-1

Figure 29-2

rawhide must be about 1" smaller than the frame in every direction. Punch 1/4" holes around the edges of the rawhide, about 2" apart, and submerge the rawhide in water overnight.

The 1/4" strip is used to attach the rawhide to the frame. Lace it very loosely at first, then work around the frame several times, removing a little slack each time. Be sure the rawhide is centered in the frame, as shown in *Figure 29-3*; if it is not, release some of the tension from the lacing, center the rawhide and pull the lacing tight again. Keep the rawhide and the rawhide strip moist during the lacing process.

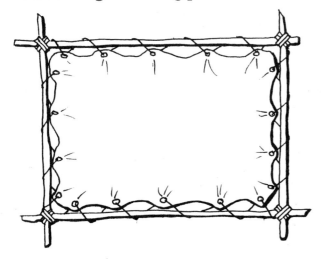

WHEN PROPERLY STRETCHED AND LACED THE RAWHIDE PANEL SHOULD ALMOST FILL THE INTERIOR OF THE FRAME

Figure 29-3

When satisfied with the appearance of rawhide and frame, set the piece aside so the rawhide may shrink. To do this, lay the totem on a flat surface, cover it with a piece of plywood and place two or three bricks or other heavy objects on the plywood while the rawhide dries and shrinks. If this is not done, the frame will warp while drying and become quite unsightly. The totem is much like a framed picture and should lay perfectly flat.

Study as many Indian drawings of animals and totems as possible before deciding on the design. Indians were excellent artists and spent a lot of time telling stories through their paintings. Find one that is pleasing to the eye and sketch it full size on a piece of paper. Remember what the totem was used for and find designs or drawings that tell a story. The photograph shown is the totem of a gentleman called *Little Gray Horse Running*; he is a member of the Turtle clan.

When satisfied with the design, transfer it to the dry rawhide using a piece of carbon paper. Use flat plastic model paints to paint the design, then decorate the totem with various natural items which also tell a story. Note the bobcat tail and deer hooves, the beaded hawk feather and beaver fur shown in the photograph; these items tell everyone Gray Horse is a successful hunter.

When finished, the totem may be displayed on a wall, hanging by a leather thong. Use plenty of imagination in deciding on the design and the decorations; the craftsperson may wish to adopt a special clan and an Indian name and display both on the totem.

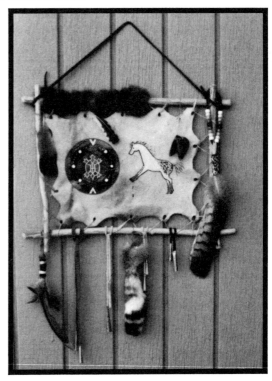

COMANCHE BUFFALO LANCE

Historians tell us the U. S. Army considered the Comanches to be the finest light cavalry in the world. Young boys became superior horsemen at the age of four or five. In their early teens, they rode with the warriors hunting buffalo and by the time they were sixteen or seventeen, they were tested warriors.

The lance was a fierce weapon used by most of the plains tribes in warfare and during the buffalo kill. Special horses were used for each; war horses were usually larger, stronger and as fearless as their riders. The horses used to chase buffalos were smaller, extremely agile and very fast.

The bow and arrow was also used in combat, but it took greater courage to get close enough to the enemy to use the lance. Since boys were taught from childhood to be brave and always display their boldness and daring, the lance was the weapon of choice.

During the hunt, the horse was trained to get his rider along the left side of the buffalo quickly so the hunter could use his lance. The hunter stabbed the buffalo behind the last rib, deep into the chest cavity where it did deadly damage to the heart and lungs. The pony then veered out of harm's way as the buffalo fell to the ground. Hunting buffalo was dangerous and many Indians were killed during the process; horses sometimes stepped in gopher holes and many were gored by a wounded buffalo. To be caught on foot in a herd of running buffalo meant certain death to the hunter.

The lance was a very special weapon surrounded by "strong medicine". The Indian's beliefs contained many superstitions and these were most evident in the lance. It is a wonderful weapon to display because of its special place in the lives of the Plains Indians, especially the Comanche.

Materials Needed

1 7', straight hardwood shaft
1 Lance head
1 24" strip of rawhide, 1/4" wide
1 48" strip of rawhide, 1/2" wide
Decorations: feathers, fur, etc.

Select a straight piece of hardwood for the lance shaft. The Indians used bois d' arc, also known as Osage Orange when it was available. The shaft is made from the trunk of a small tree, no taller that twelve or fourteen feet. The small end of the shaft should be about 1" in diameter and the butt end of the shaft about 2" in diameter. All branches and bark must be removed and the shaft set aside to dry and cure. Bois d'

arc is extremely hard wood and difficult to work; any hard wood works well for the replica. Be careful when working with the knife and always cut away from the body!

In the early days, the head of the spear was made of cherp, flint or sometimes obsidian. When the trappers brought iron to the mountains, the Indians quickly replaced the stone heads with spear heads made of metal. If the craftsperson is experienced

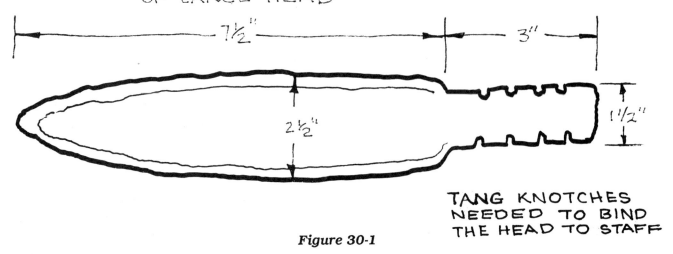

TYPICAL SIZE AND SHAPE
OF LANCE HEAD

7½"

3"

2½"

1½"

TANG KNOTCHES
NEEDED TO BIND
THE HEAD TO STAFF

Figure 30-1

and has access to a blacksmith's forge, hammer and anvil, a lance head may be made from scratch; the general shape and dimensions are given in *Figure 30-1*. However, many lance head reproductions are on the market and make this step unnecessary. The author purchased an iron head to make the lance shown in the photograph. Unless the craftsperson is experienced in working with iron, the purchase of a manufactured lance head is highly recommended.

When the shaft is completely cured, sand it smooth and coat the wood with a 50-50 mixture of linseed oil and turpentine. Cut a 3" notch in the small end, as shown in *Figure 30-2*, to accept the lance head.

Soak the rawhide strips in water for several hours, then insert the head into the notched shaft and wrap the joint with the 1/4" wet rawhide strip, in the manner illustrated in *Figure 30-3*.

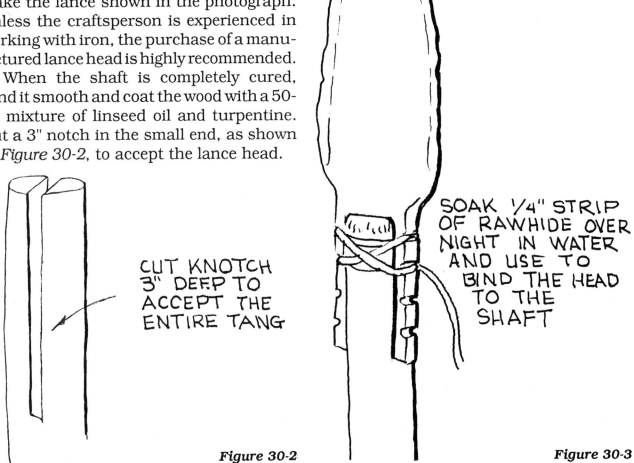

CUT KNOTCH
3" DEEP TO
ACCEPT THE
ENTIRE TANG

SOAK 1/4" STRIP
OF RAWHIDE OVER
NIGHT IN WATER
AND USE TO
BIND THE HEAD
TO THE
SHAFT

Figure 30-2

Figure 30-3

Use the 1/2" rawhide strip to wrap around the shaft as a handle as shown in *Figure 30-4).*

The shaft is now ready for decoration. Rabbit fur, feathers, barrel beads, etc. are suitable for this purpose. Remember, this item is a replica of a deadly weapon. It is sharp and dangerous and should be treated with great care. This is not a toy, it is a weapon. Treat it as such.

SOAK 1/2" RAWHIDE STRIP AND WRAP AROUND STAFF TO FORM HANDLE

Figure 30-4

MINICONJOU DANCE RATTLE

The tribal dance and sing was a part of all Indian cultures and religions. They danced to celebrate the coming of spring, they danced prior to an approaching battle and they performed a ceremonial dance before the buffalo hunt. They celebrated their triumphs and conquests after battles and sometimes they sang and danced simply for the joy of life. Young braves found wives during tribal dances. All members of the tribe joined in the festivities, dancing and singing to the music provided by the tom-tom and flute. Individuals enjoyed keeping time to the rhythm by shaking a dance rattle.

Rattles came in all sizes and shapes; some examples are given in *Figure 31-1*. They were made from many different materials, depending on what was available at the time.

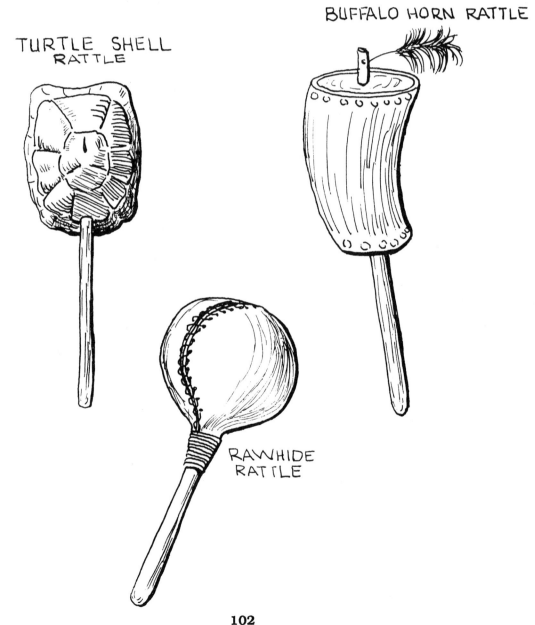

TURTLE SHELL RATTLE

BUFFALO HORN RATTLE

RAWHIDE RATTLE

Figure 31-1

102

The head of this rattle is made from a 3" diameter x 1" thick slab of a tree limb (*Figure 31-2*). Remove the inner part of this slab with a wood drill or chisel and hammer. Be careful when removing the wood from the center of the rattle head, chisels and drills make nasty wounds. Leave about a 1/2" rim of wood around the outside, as shown in *Figure 31-3*. Drill a 1/2" hole for the handle in the rim and sand the outside edges to eliminate the sharp edges.

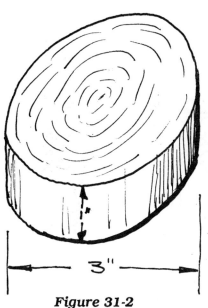

Figure 31-2

The handle is made from a 14" length of a 1/2" diameter branch. Remove all the leaves and bark from the handle, round one end with sand paper and glue it into the rim, as illustrated in *Figure 31-4*.

Figure 31-4

Cut the two pieces of rawhide into circles about 1/2" larger in diameter than the rim. Place one piece of rawhide on a work bench and use an awl to carefully punch a series of holes around the edge of the rawhide, about 1/4" from the outer edge (see *Figure 31-5*). When finished, do the same with the other piece of rawhide. Place both pieces of rawhide in warm water and leave overnight.

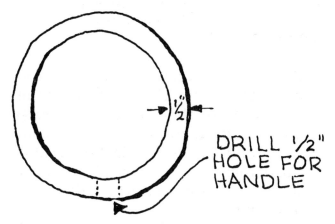

Figure 31-3

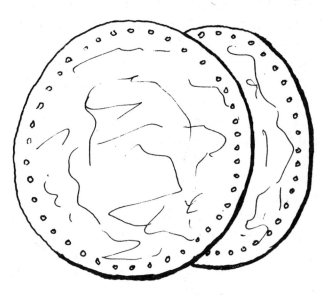

Figure 31-5

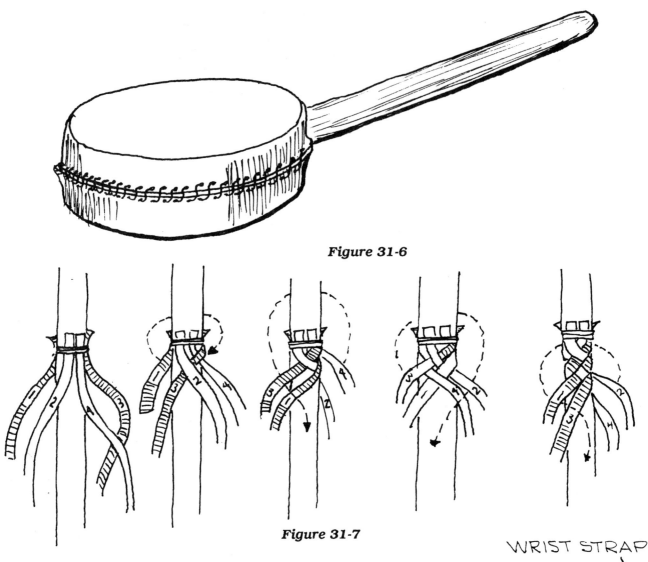

Figure 31-6

Figure 31-7

Begin lacing the two pieces of rawhide around the rattle head (see *Figure 31-6*). Place the small stones or beads inside the rattle before completing the lacing. Keep the rawhide wet during this lacing process. Set the rattle aside overnight and allow the rawhide to dry and shrink.

Cut both pieces of ribbon in half, creating four pieces of equal length. Attach the ribbons to the handle, next to the rattle head. Weave them around the handle as diagrammed in *Figure 31-7*.

Whip stitch the felt around the lower end of the handle for a better grip and for the color it adds. Drill a 1/8" hole in the end of the handle for the sinew wrist strap and attach it as shown in *Figure 31-8*.

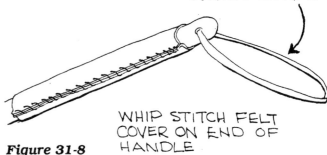

WRIST STRAP

WHIP STITCH FELT COVER ON END OF HANDLE

Figure 31-8

The handle can now be decorated with beads, feathers, etc. The last step is painting the faces of the rattle. The design should be much like other parfleche paintings, bold and simple. Use flat finish paints obtained from stores that sell plastic model paints. Do not use paint which dries with a glossy finish.

KIOWA ANTLER HANDLE KNIFE

One of the most useful antler projects is the knife handle. The knife was one tool almost every Indian and mountain man used. Women carried knives to butcher buffalo, to cut food for cooking and to protect themselves in emergencies. Indian men used their knives for hunting and fighting and trappers needed a good sharp knife every day they were in the mountains.

Before the white man entered the plains, most Indian knives were made of napped or chipped flint or obsidian. The handles were usually just a piece of wet rawhide wrapped around the blunt end of the stone knife (see *Figure 32-1*).

The white man brought steel knife blades from the east; one of the best was the Green River knife, made by John Russell and Company, located on the banks of the Green

River near Deerfield, Massachusetts (see *Figure 32-2*). The Indians liked the knives of the trappers and the Green River made a handsome trade item.

Even the best knives had hardwood handles and many times the wood cracked and broke off the blades, making the knife useless until the handle could be repaired. There were many materials to use - many replaced the handle with a buffalo bone and some used a piece of a tree limb, but the most attractive replacement handles were made of deer antlers. Large knives needed a mule deer or elk antler, while white-tailed deer antlers worked fine for smaller blades.

The antler-handled knife is a beautiful item and makes a nice addition to any collection.

Figure 32-1

J. RUSSEL & CO.
GREEN RIVER WORKS

Figure 32-2

Materials Needed

1   4-5 inch piece of antler taken from the corona end.
1   Paring knife blade (any small blade will do).
    Epoxy glue

Cut the antler and round the edges with a file as indicated in *Figure 32-3*. Sand the hilt end of the handle as smooth as possible, using ever finer grit and finishing with #400 sand paper and water.

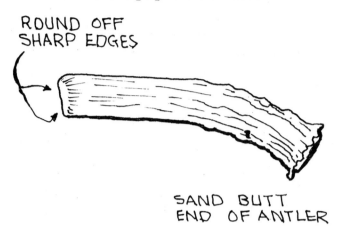

ROUND OFF SHARP EDGES

SAND BUTT END OF ANTLER

Figure 32-3

The shank of the knife blade must be ground as shown in *Figure 32-4*. There are two reasons to be careful during the grinding process. First, it's easy to receive a nasty cut and second, if the blade turns blue from too much heat, the metal has lost its temper and will not hold an edge. An electric sand paper disc is recommended for this process as it removes metal more slowly than a grinding stone and allows the blade to hold its hard temper. When the blade is approximately the shape of the diagram set the blade aside and return to the antler handle.

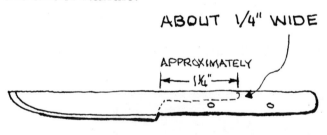

ABOUT 1/4" WIDE

APPROXIMATELY 1¼"

REMOVE EXCESS METAL FROM SHANK

Figure 32-4

For safety, clamp the handle in a vise and then drill a 1/8" pilot hole in the hilt end of the handle, as illustrated in *Figure 32-5*. Drill this hole very carefully; make sure the angle of the drill will not result in a hole through the outer wall of the handle. If this happens, the antler is ruined. The pilot hole should be as deep as the shank on the knife blade. Now enlarge the pilot hole with a 1/4" drill bit.

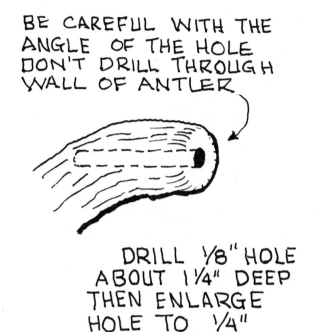

BE CAREFUL WITH THE ANGLE OF THE HOLE DON'T DRILL THROUGH WALL OF ANTLER

DRILL 1/8" HOLE ABOUT 1¼" DEEP THEN ENLARGE HOLE TO 1/4"

Figure 32-5

Place the knife shank in the hole and check for depth and angle of the blade to the handle. If adjustments are required, either grind off more of the blade or enlarge the hole with the drill. Several adjustments will probably be needed before the craftsperson is completely happy with the angle of the blade and the overall appearance of the knife. It is much better to make several small adjustments rather than one big one. Too big an adjustment may ruin the project.

As soon as the correct appearance is achieved, mix 2-part epoxy glue and fill the hole in the handle. A small wire may need to be inserted from time to time while filling the hole to keep air pockets from forming in the handle. Coat both sides of the hilt of the blade completely with epoxy, as shown in *Figure 32-6*. Insert the knife blade into the

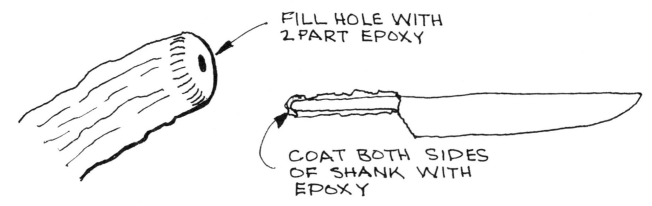

FILL HOLE WITH 2 PART EPOXY

COAT BOTH SIDES OF SHANK WITH EPOXY

Figure 32-6

hole. Use a clean rag to wipe off all over-run epoxy on the handle and blade, align it properly and set it aside until the epoxy has set. Working and setting times for epoxy vary, so read the instructions on the epoxy containers.

After the epoxy has set, take a look at the knife. There will probably be space around the knife blade and the hole in the handle, as indicated in *Figure 32-7*. This is easily filled with a product called *Bondo*; which is the compound used by automobile body repairmen. It's an ideal filler for all sorts of projects; it files and sands easily and cures with a natural color. Mix a bit of hardener with a small portion of Bondo and fill the space around the knife blade. Wipe off the excess, set the knife aside and allow the Bondo to cure.

If an aged finish is desired on the handle, submerge the handle in stale, cold coffee or tea for a few hours. Then buff slightly with extra fine steel wool.

Use this new knife with caution, sharp blades cut anything from wood to fingers;

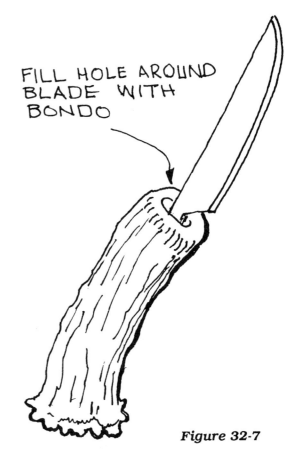

FILL HOLE AROUND BLADE WITH BONDO

Figure 32-7

the knife doesn't know the difference!

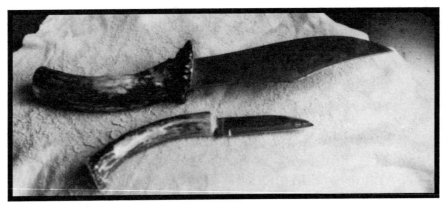

MOUNTAIN MAN RIFLE CASE

A trapper's best friend was his rifle, he carried it with him at all times. It was a special relationship that went far beyond that of today's hunters and their favorite weapon. The mountain man's life depended on his rifle and this fact led many to give their rifles special names. Some were named after long lost girlfriends and others were named for the weapon's ability to shoot straight and bring down game.

The favorite rifle among trappers was made by Jake and Samuel Hawken. The Hawken Gun Shop was located at 214 N. Main Street in St. Louis. The brothers modified the Kentucky rifle; the barrel was shortened but was made considerably heavier. The stock was cut off and extended only halfway down the barrel. The .53 caliber was the most common, but many different sizes were available, up to .58 caliber. Some were fitted with flintlock and others were percussion cap.

To protect something as special as his rifle, the mountain man crafted a beautiful, elk skin rifle case. It usually was fringed on the bottom side and often decorated with beads and sometimes fur. A good rifle case was necessary to keep the weapon clean and dry. Smoking elk skin waterproofed the material and made it a very good material for their rifle cases.

Materials Needed

1   Piece of elk or buck skin big enough to cover both
      sides of the rifle, leaving a bit over for fringe
1   10' sinew
1   12" tieing thong
1   Piece of heavy wrapping paper for pattern
    Beads, fur, feathers, etc. for decoration.

First, lay the wrapping paper on a flat surface and then lay the rifle on the paper (see *Figure 33-1*). Trace the outline of the rifle on the paper, then fold the paper creasing it along the top line of the barrel, as indicated by the dotted line in *Figure 33-2*. Use a pair of scissors to cut both the top and bottom sides of the pattern at the same time (follow the traced outline). Place the paper pattern on the elk skin and use scissors to cut out the rifle case. When cutting the case be sure to add three or four inches on the bottom side of the case for fringe and about six inches on one side of

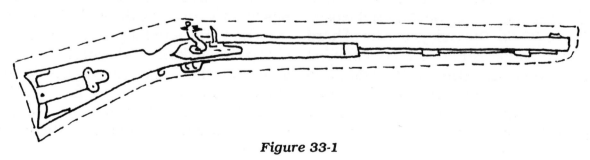

Figure 33-1

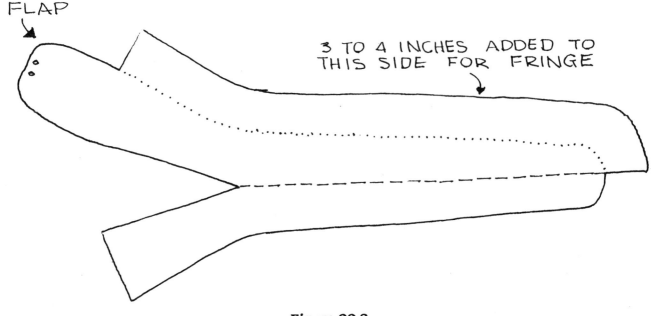

FLAP

3 TO 4 INCHES ADDED TO THIS SIDE FOR FRINGE

Figure 33-2

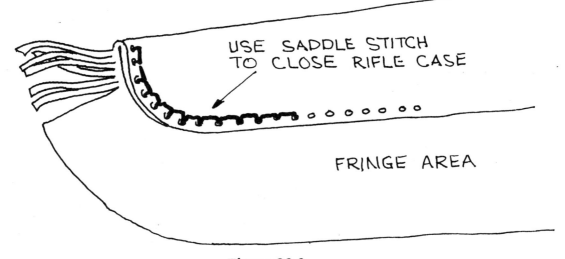

AFTER CASE IS COMPLETELY STITCHED, CAREFULLY CUT THE FRINGE

USE SADDLE STITCH TO CLOSE RIFLE CASE

FRINGE AREA

Figure 33-3

the large (stock) end for the closing flap.

Use two sharp harness needles and sinew to stitch the bottom of the material closed (see *Figure 33-3*). The case gets a lot of hard use so the saddle stitch is recommended (this stitch is illustrated in the *Mountain Man Ball Bag* project, *Figure 7-2*). The rifle should fit snugly in the case, but the case must also be wide enough for the rifle to slip into

and out of the case easily. It may be easier to use an awl to punch the holes before passing the needles through the leather.

When the stitching is finished, use a sharp Exacto knife and a straight edge as a guide for the knife, to cut the fringe as shown in *Figure 33-3*. The finer the fringe is cut, the more handsome the case will be. Be very careful when cutting the fringe; a sharp blade cuts fingers as easily as it cuts elk skin!

Set the case aside and decide what type of decoration is to be added. Some may not wish to embellish their case and will leave it as is. But mountain men enjoyed living with the Indians and often copied their craftsmanship by decorating their rifle cases with beads, feathers and pieces of fur. A decorated gun case makes a handsome item and taking this final step is highly recommended.

If a beaded decoration is desired, the easiest and quickest way to produce a beautiful design is to make it on a bead loom and stitch the finished band on the side of the case. See the *Plains Indian Beadwork* project near the beginning of this book for beading techniques. As an alternative, already beaded strips can often be purchased at trading posts or through mail order catalogs.

When the beaded band is complete, stitch it to the side of the case as indicated in *Figure 33-4*. Other decorations, such as feathers, shells or pieces of fur, can be added as desired at this time.

The flap on the large end of the case is now ready for a twelve inch thong, as shown in *Figure 33-5*. Use a leather punch for the holes. Place the rifle in the case, fold the flap over and tie the thong around the case. The mountain man rifle case is now complete and ready for the next hunting season!

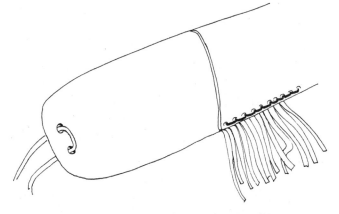

PLACE RIFLE IN CASE FOLD FLAP OVER AND TIE SHUT WITH THONG

Figure 33-5

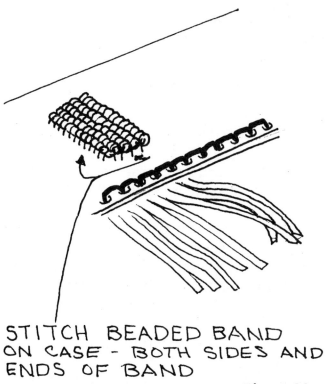

STITCH BEADED BAND ON CASE - BOTH SIDES AND ENDS OF BAND

Figure 33-4

OKLAHOMA PLAINS INDIAN FLUTE

The Indians believed everything had a spirit; animate or inanimate, since it was made by the great one above, it had to have a spirit. Even music had a spirit. Music has an effect on everyone and everything; it helps makes us the people we are.

The flute was first created to duplicate the sounds of birds. It was used at all dance celebrations and during the healing rituals of the medicine man. It also had strong medicine in love affairs; young men played strange and haunting melodies to charm the young girls of their dreams.

Genuine Indian flutes are difficult to find, even in museums. One reason for this may be tribal beliefs. As an example, a Comanche made and owned only one flute during his lifetime; when he died, the flute was buried with him.

It is good for the soul to make an Indian flute. There is an Indian story about a lonely orphan who received a flute from the Great Spirit. As the Spirit presented his gift, he told the boy, "As long as you have this flute, you will always be comforted by the music from it. Get your sounds from the woods and you will always find good music." There is truly something magical about the subtle, exotic tones from the flute. Maybe the Indians were right, perhaps the flute has a spirit.

The Indian flute most familiar to Americans came from the Apaches of New Mexico. Most of their flutes were made from mahogany but cedar is preferred by today's flute makers.

Materials Needed

2 Pieces of wood, 3/4" x 1 1/2" x 24"
    (white pine works well)
1 Piece of tin 1/2" x 1 1/4 "
    (used for the "nest")
1 Piece of wood, 3/8" x 1 1/4" x 2"
    (used for the "bird")
Decorative materials as desired.

Cut duplicate slots down the length of both pieces of wood, as shown in *Figure 34-1*. These slots will form the central wind tube of the flute. A small obstruction, about 1/8" thick (something like the node in a cane pole), is needed in the tube. Place it in the slot, one hand's width from the end of the flute which will become the mouthpiece. This obstruction must block off the entire tube and allow no air to pass.

Glue the two pieces of wood together using white wood glue. Do not glue the obstruction and keep track of its position. Set the flute aside and allow the glue to dry completely.

When the glue is dry, use a pocket knife and carefully carve the body of the flute until it is completely round, with a point on the mouthpiece end (the obstruction end). Sand the body smooth, using finer grits of sand paper and ending with 400 grit.

Locate the obstruction and drill a hole on either side of it, then carve the holes square. Next carve away and flatten the

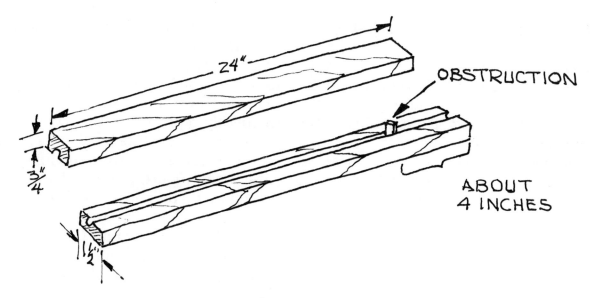

Figure 34-1

wood around the two square holes, as indicated in *Figure 34-2*. This area is called the "roost".

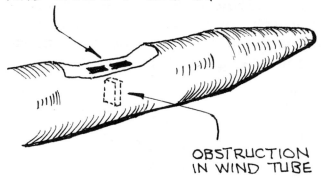

FLATTEN AREA, DRILL HOLES ON EACH SIDE OF THE OBSTRUCTION AND CARVE HOLES SQUARE

OBSTRUCTION IN WIND TUBE

Figure 34-2

Grasp the flute and place the mouthpiece end in the mouth. Place the first three fingers of each hand on the body of the flute, one hand below the other, so that the grip is comfortable. Mark the location of each finger. Drill a 1/4" tone hole at each mark, as illustrated in *Figure 34-3*. These holes are not drilled in a straight line but in arcs to fit the players' fingers.

To give the flute a proper finish, "whiskering" the wood is recommended. After a thorough sanding, when the body is as smooth as possible, moisten it with a damp rag. As the wood dries, small "whiskers" will stand up on the surface of the wood. Remove them with very fine sand paper and repeat this process until no more

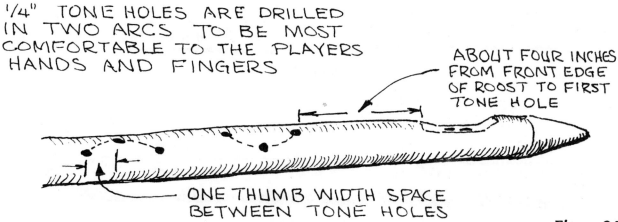

1/4" TONE HOLES ARE DRILLED IN TWO ARCS TO BE MOST COMFORTABLE TO THE PLAYERS HANDS AND FINGERS

ABOUT FOUR INCHES FROM FRONT EDGE OF ROOST TO FIRST TONE HOLE

ONE THUMB WIDTH SPACE BETWEEN TONE HOLES

Figure 34-3

"whiskers" appear.

Stain the body of the flute as desired and hand rub several coats of 1/2 turpentine and 1/2 linseed oil solution into the wood. Set the flute aside and allow it to dry for 24 hours, then rub a few more coats of the solution into the wood. This should give the wood a great finish.

Cut the small piece of tin or *nest*, as indicated in *Figure 34-4* and fit it to the flattened wood area or "roost".

APPROXIMATE SHAPE OF NEST, CUT TO FIT THE ROOST SO THE HOLES OF THE NEST MATCH THE HOLES OF THE ROOST.

Figure 34-4

It is now time to carve the "bird". *Figure 34-5* shows various designs for the "bird" or the craftsperson may wish to design an original. The small block of wood is carved to represent a bird or an animal and mounted over the windway. The "bird" frequently represented the owner's clan.

Assemble the flute by placing the "nest" on the "roost" and setting the "bird" on the "nest" (see *Figure 34-6*). Use a strip of buckskin to tie these three components together.

Apache, Choctaw and Creek flutes had three tone holes, the Sioux flutes had five. Flutes made by the Oklahoma Plains Indians were made with six tone holes and became the standard for all Indian flutes. Flutes are as individual as the people who make them. The author has made several, some of which will not make any tone whatsoever. When this happens, Indian friends tell him to throw them away, but he never does. Making flutes is like that, sometimes the magic works and sometimes it doesn't. But this should not hinder the craftsperson; if the flute won't make music, it still looks great hanging on the wall.

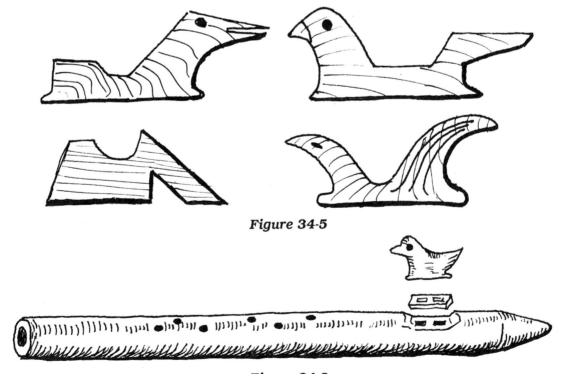

Figure 34-5

Figure 34-6

114

No one can teach another how to play an Indian flute, crafters and players have to teach themselves. It takes a lot of time and practice to make the beautiful tones and longer to compose a song. But remember, when the tune is played it is the first time the world has ever heard that exact sound!

Feel free to decorate the flute with feathers, beads, strips of buckskin, rawhide or feather fluffs.

HORN HAT RACK

Horns can be used for a great many projects. When properly polished and presented, they are truly attractive. A hat rack is a useful item, easy to make and is a handsome addition to a den or entry way.

Raw horns are usually ugly items when first obtained. A great deal of work is required to rid them of all the natural roughness. A rasp file is recommended to remove most of the rugged surface. When that's all removed, sand paper is then applied. Start with coarse paper and continue with finer and finer grit, finally finishing with 600 grit used with water. The appearance of a polished horn is beautiful; it becomes translucent and has great depth.

Next, cut off the large, ragged ends of the horns, as shown in *Figure 35-1*. Place each horn on one of the 4" x 4" blocks and trace around the horns with a pencil (see *Figure 35-2*). Use a coping saw or band saw to cut out the round wood discs thus marked. If power tools are used, be sure and observe all the safety rules.

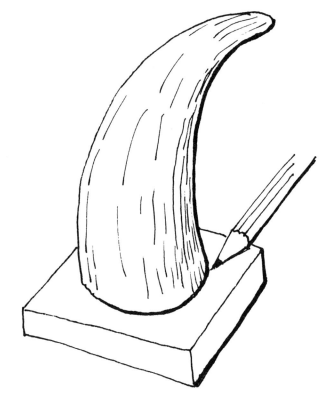

TRACE THE OUTLINE OF THE HORN ON THE BLOCK OF WOOD

Figure 35-2

With the rasp file, file the sides of each disc to approximate the angle on the inside of its respective horn (see *Figure 35-3*). Each disc should be slightly larger than its horn.

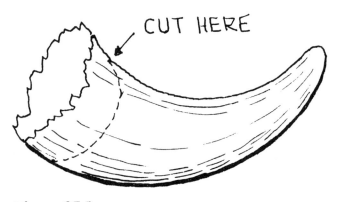

CUT HERE

Figure 35-1

116

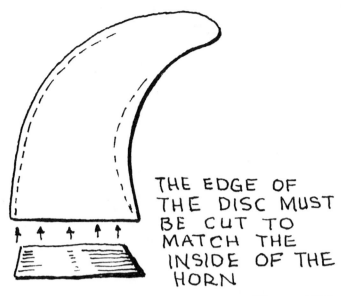

THE EDGE OF THE DISC MUST BE CUT TO MATCH THE INSIDE OF THE HORN

Figure 35-3

If too much wood is removed with the file, the horn will slip on the disc. If this happens, simply use epoxy to attach the horn to the disc. Make sure that the outside of the disc is flush with the end of the horn.

It is better if the wood disc starts into the horn but stops before it is fully seated. In this case, use the following procedure to attach the disc.

Place about three inches of water in a large sauce pan and set it on the stove. Bring the water to a rolling boil and using a baker's mitt, insert the large end of the horn into the water. Use extreme care in this process. Burns caused by steam and hot water are severe! The hot water will soften the horn and make it pliable. After the horn has been in the boiling water for a few minutes, put the disc on a surface by the side of the stove and carefully place the horn on the disc. It should slip down over the disc and the edges of the horn should be flush with the outside of the disc.

Set the horns aside to cool and shrink around the wood. If the process is done properly, the wood disc will be securely "welded" to the horn.

No further finishing should be needed, however if there are water spots on the horn, they can be easily removed by sand-ing with 600 grit sand paper used with cool water.

Use sand paper to put an attractive finish on the 12" x 36" mounting board. Take plenty of time during this process. Some craftspeople get in a hurry when working with wood and this leads to a sloppily finished project. Any wood can be used for the mounting board; pine, birch or if a nice texture is desired, ash, are all recommended. Various trims are available to finish the edges of the mounting board, if this is desired; rope may even be used to add an unusual finish to the outside of this project (see *Figure 35-4*).

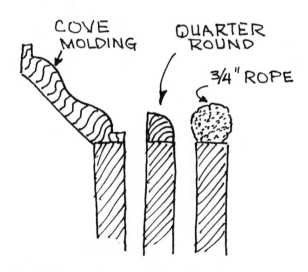

COVE MOLDING   QUARTER ROUND

3/4" ROPE

VARIOUS MATERIALS CAN BE USED TO TRIM EDGE OF MOUNTING BOARD

Figure 35-4

Attach the horns to the mounting board by drilling pilot holes through the back of the board, as shown in *Figure 35-5*. Center the horns over the holes, then use a good grade of wood glue and 1 1/2" wood screws to secure the horns to the mounting board.

There are various types of hangers available to tack to the back of the mounting board which will allow the finished hat rack to hang on the wall. Select the one that best serves the purpose and install it on the back of the board. Congratulations! There is now a place to hang that mountain man hat or war bonnet!

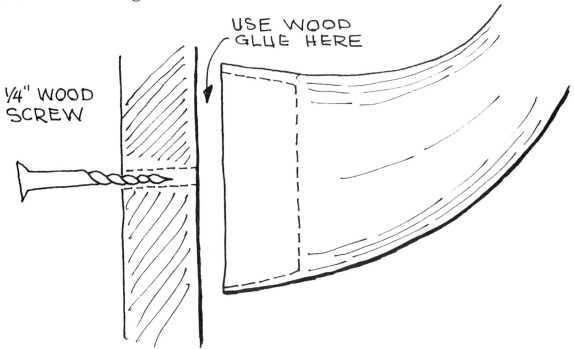

Figure 35-5

INDIAN CLOTH DYE

The American Indian liked color; a glance at Navaho blankets and it is easy to understand that love affair. The Pueblo Indians made and dyed cotton clothing as early as 1540. Some archaeologists date the first cloth woven as early as 700 A. D. The Navaho began weaving in the 1700's and by the early 1800's Navaho wool blankets were a highly regarded trade item at the mountain man rendezvous.

The Indians used plants to make their dyes. Some of the native plants they used were: Several-Flowered and Single-Flowered Actinea, Alder, Rocky Mountain Bee Plant, Bitterball, Prickly Pear Cactus, Canyaigre, Wild Celery, Chamizo, Chokecherry, Owl's Claw, Oregon Grape, Ironwood or Wild Privet, One-Seeded Juniper, Wild Purple Larkspur, Ground Lichen, Blue-Flowered Lupine, Mountain Mahogany, Gambel's Oak, Indian Paintbrush, Scrub Oak, Wild Plum, Pinedrop, Small Rabbitbrush, Big Rabbitbrush and Russian Thistle.

These plants do not grow in all parts of the country but the interested craftsperson may still enjoy making natural dyes and dyeing cotton and wool from many products found in the family garden or grocery store:

- Carrot tops create a lime green color.
- The outer skin of dried onions produces a bright orange dye.
- Tomato leaves result in a medium green.
- Twigs from an apple tree provide a yellow-orange.
- Blackberries produce a rose or pink.
- Fresh beets make a beautiful tan dye.
- Blueberries create a pale blue color.
- Purple cabbage also makes a beautiful blue.

Materials Needed

1   Knife
1   Chopping board
    Fruits, vegetables or trimmings (see above)
    Alum
    Fruit jars, cheese cloth & stirring stick

Dyeing is not easy and it takes a lot of experimenting to satisfy some craftspeople. The size of the jar depends on the size of the material to be dyed and the amount of plant material used to make the dye varies greatly. Colors can not be duplicated; each time a dye is made, it produces a slightly different color, so dye more material than it seems will be needed.

Use only pure cotton or wool; man-made fabrics do not absorb natural dyes easily and produce disappointing results.

Find a place, preferably outdoors to make the dye. It can be messy and the finished dye will stain almost anything it touches, including the kitchen sink. Chop the plant material into small pieces and place it in a glass jar, then fill the jar with fresh water and set it outside. Be careful with that knife; a cut finger is not much fun!

The mixture should sit in hot sunshine for two to three days before it is used. Using cheese cloth, carefully strain off the vegetable matter and save the liquid. Raw dye fades if used at this stage; a "fixing" agent is needed before it is used. A teaspoon or two of alum works great for this purpose and assures the colors remain bright for years.

Dampen the material to be dyed thoroughly with water before it is placed in the jar. If yarn is to be dyed, wind it into loose skeins and be sure it is completely damp before placing it in the solution. Use the stirring stick to assure all the material is submerged in the liquid. Put a lid on the jar and set it back in the sun for a day or two. Plant dyes produce softer colors than commercial ones and take longer to work. Check the jar each day; remember the material will appear darker when it's wet and will be lighter when it dries. Use the stirring stick to remove the material from the solution. The last step is a thorough rinsing of the material with a garden hose. Continue rinsing until the water runs clear and then hang the material in the shade to dry.

INDIAN GAMES

Most Anglos believe the American Indians were sullen, mean bloodthirsty folk with no sense of humor; people who entertained themselves with continuous warring raids against their enemies. Quite to the contrary, most of the Plains tribes were made up of average people, much like those found in any small city in the United States today.

True, the Indians of the early 1800's had several cultural differences from people in the United States today. One of the major differences was the loyalty of the Indians to one another; the need to "stick together" was not only a cultural thing, it was necessary for survival. Each and every member of the village was important to the village. Family bonds were most important, followed by allegiance to the band, and finally to the tribe. If war was necessary, every able-bodied man, whose "medicine" was right, answered the call and protected the people, with his life if required.

But warfare was not practiced as often as modern day movies would lead us to believe. Indians delighted in being together and enjoying each other. They often played practical jokes on one another and played many social games. Two of the most widely played games are the subject of this project.

THE WHEEL AND STICK GAME

The Wheel (or Hoop) and Stick Game was played by members of the men's societies. A challenge between societies was presented and accepted. The playing field was a level piece of ground about thirty feet long with a log, or goal, placed at each end of the course. Each society selected a player and after singing ritual songs, the game began. Spectators lined the playing field to watch the proceedings.

The wheel was used as a moving target. A small hoop was laced inside the outer wheel and served as the bull's-eye. The wheel and hoop were laced together with rawhide spokes and the spokes were decorated with different colored beads. Each of the players used an arrow-like lance which was about three feet long, with an arrow head and feathering.

One of the players rolled the wheel toward a goal while the other attempted to throw a lance though the small hoop. Then the other player took a turn. The first to hit the target was named winner.

> **Materials Needed**
>
> 1 Wheel, approx. 12" in diameter
> 1 Hoop, approx. 4" in diameter
> 1 1/2" x 36" willow branch or dowel
>   Rawhide for wrapping and spokes
>   Beads for decoration of wheel
>   Arrow head and feathers for lance

The local hobby shop will usually have several sizes of wooden hoops available - these are recommended, but if not available, the wheel and hoop can be made from willow branches.

If willow branches are used, remove the bark. The thickness of the willow branch dictates the diameter of the finished hoop; the smaller the diameter of the branch, the tighter it will bend and the smaller the finished hoop will be. Bend the wheel limb slowly, working from one end to the other several times to complete the circle. Bending the branch too fast will certainly break the wood and the process will have to be started again.

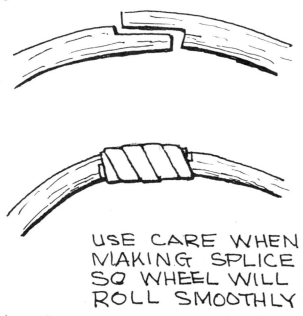

USE CARE WHEN MAKING SPLICE SO WHEEL WILL ROLL SMOOTHLY

Figure 37-1

Figure 37-1 shows how to notch the ends and bind them together to finish the wheel. The wheel must roll easily so it has to be as round as possible. When the wheel is finished, start with a smaller branch and use the same process to complete the inner hoop. When both hoops are finished, set them aside until they have dried completely. Willow tends to shrink as it dries, so do not proceed with construction until the wooden hoops are completely cured. Sand the outside of the large hoop so it will roll smoothly across the floor.

Cut strips of rawhide and place them in water overnight. Wrap the wheel and hoop with the rawhide, as indicated in Figure 37-2, and set them aside to dry.

WRAP WHEEL AND HOOP WITH WET RAWHIDE

Figure 37-2

When both the wheel and hoop are dry, use wet rawhide to connect the two with a series of rawhide spokes. If desired, thread colored barrel beads on the spokes during this process. For the wheel to roll true, the hoop must be carefully centered in the wheel, as illustrated in Figure 37-3. Give the wheel added strength by connecting the spokes with another strip of rawhide and the wheel is finished.

To build the lance, a straight willow branch or a 1/2" wooden dowel is needed. Strip the bark if a branch is used and notch one end of the shaft. Install the arrow head as shown in Figure 37-4, using sinew to attach the arrow head to the shaft.

Next, attach the feathers to the opposite end of the lance as indicated in Figure 37-5. Use thread and white glue to secure the feathers to the shaft. Allow the glue to dry.

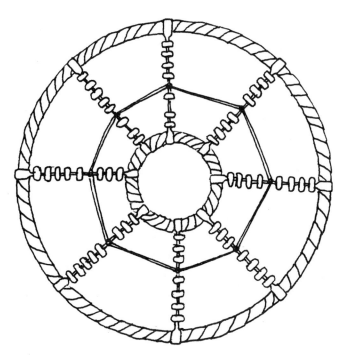

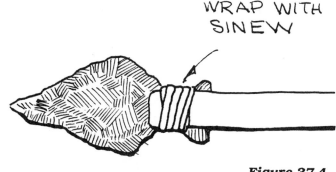

WRAP WITH SINEW

Figure 37-4

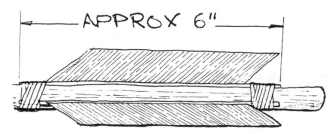

← APPROX 6" →

SIDE VIEW

IN ASSEMBLY, CENTER THE HOOP WITHIN THE WHEEL, USE BARREL BEADS TO DECORATE THE SPOKES IF DESIRED.

Figure 37-3

The Wheel and Stick Game implements are now complete and ready for use; it takes a bit of practice to hit the rolling hoop. Remember, this "game" also had a practical use. While playing, the Indians honed skills necessary for successfully killing a buffalo. Good players always hit the hoop after two or three tries. Give it a try!

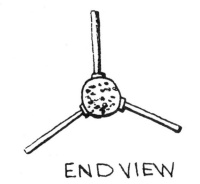

END VIEW

Figure 37-5

HAND GAME

This game was played by everyone. It was much like the Anglo game, "Button, button, whose got the button?". The Blackfeet called it Fancy Gambling. Men used pieces of bone small enough to be completely hidden in a clenched fist; women and children used peach seeds. One bone or peach seed was unmarked and the other one had small spots painted on both sides.

Players sat facing each other and the hands of the player hiding the objects were moved back and forth in front of the opponent. During this display, the pieces were passed from hand to hand in an attempt to confuse the rival player. At the appropriate time, the player with the pieces stopped and the opposing player guessed which hand held the marked object. If the challenger guessed wrong, one point was awarded to the player hiding the objects and that person continued to hide the items. If the guess was right the challenger

123

was awarded a point and won a turn at hiding the pieces. Twelve short willow sticks were used as counters and the first to win all twelve counters was declared the winner of the game. Indians loved to gamble and played this game as a social outlet from youth to old age.

Materials Needed

2   Small bones or peach seeds
12 6" pieces of willow branch, 3/8" diameter
    Red, flat paint and small brush

The bones must be free of all flesh, sinew, etc.; boiling the bones will remove such material. If peach seeds are used, they must be free of all fruit residue and completely dry. With a small paint brush, daub two or three spots on both sides of one of the tokens. Use paint with a flat finish, such as that used on plastic models.

Cut twelve counters, then round off and sand smooth the ends to eliminate any splinters. If desired, the counters may be decorated with paint; use flat-finish paint for this process; the Indians used natural products for their painted decorations and these colors dried with a flat, not glossy finish.

Find a friend and while away the hours with this wonderful Indian game!

LAKOTA BEAR AMULET

The Plains Indians were spiritual people. Their religion was primitive by today's Anglo standards, but it served them well. Indian religion was based on natural things; things they could see and touch. Their supreme being was called by various names but a general translation of the individual tribal names could be Maker of All. Their religion was real and meaningful to the Indians because it was attached to living objects such as birds and animals.

The buffalo was a sacred animal in Indian religion because it provided so many things the Indians used. The eagle was a revered bird; strong and powerful, the king of the sky was a constant source of spiritual guidance. The wolf was worshipped because of it's strength and endurance and the bear was held in high esteem because of it's power and courage.

An amulet is something worn on the body because of its magic power to keep the wearer from injury or evil. The Indians created many religious amulets and carried them to provide protection. In a small way, an amulet could be compared to a good luck charm, such as a rabbit's foot, but they served a much stronger purpose. Each amulet was filled with special "medicine" that was counted on for the security and protection it offered to the wearer.

The subject for this project is the grizzly bear, the strongest and most courageous beast of the Rocky Mountains. Few, if any, tribes ever hunted or killed the grizzly; it was treated with respect and reverence.

Materials Needed

1   2" x 3" x 3/4" block of clear, white pine
    Wood finishing materials
    Materials for a carry pouch
        (buckskin, sinew, leather thong)

Figure 38-1

USE FOR FULL SIZE PATTERN. AS LAST STEP, PAINT LIGHTNING ON BOTH SIDES OF FINISHED AMULET.

Using the pattern given in *Figure 38-1*, trace the outline of the bear onto the side of the block of wood. Since the block of wood is so small, it is a good idea to clamp the block onto the edge of a workbench with a C clamp before beginning to saw. Using a coping saw, or band saw if available, carefully cut out the bear. Extreme care should be exercised when using any kind of a saw, especially a band saw.

The next step is to use a sharp pocket knife. Always pay close attention to the task when using a knife and push the blade away from the body when whittling. Follow the instructions in *Figure 38-2* and remove

Figure 38-2

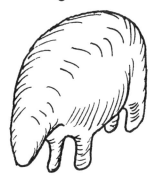

USE A SHARP KNIFE OR DREMIL TOOL WITH A SANDING DRUM TO REMOVE EXCESS WOOD. THE AMULET IS STYLIZED ART -- LET ALL CURVES FLOW INTO ONE ANOTHER.

the excess wood until the desired results are achieved. Sand the amulet carefully until it is as smooth as possible.

A good product to use while finishing the project is Sanding Sealer, available from your local model airplane outlet. Thoroughly cover the bear with a good coat of sanding sealer, set aside to dry, then sand with 400 grit sand paper. The more coats of sealer applied and sanded, the smoother the wood will become.

When satisfied with the overall appearance, the bear should be painted with flat brown or black paint. Several coats of paint will also enhance the overall appearance of the amulet. The last step is applying the blue lightning streak. This design should be painted on both sides.

Indians carried their amulets in small buckskin pouches, usually strung around their necks with a strong leather thong. The bags were very plain, see *Figure 38-3*, with no decoration. The craftsperson may wish to carry the pouch in a pocket. Always remember to keep the medicine bear amulet near and no evil will come your way!

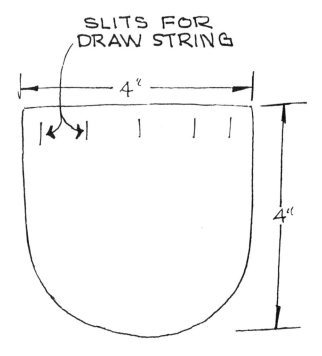

SLITS FOR DRAW STRING

4"

4"

TWO IDENTICAL PIECES OF BUCKSKIN ARE NEEDED. FOR COMPLETE INSTRUCTIONS FOR AMULET POUCH SEE THE MOUNTAIN MAN BALL BAG PROJECT

Figure 38-3

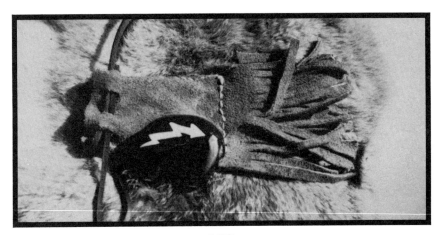

PISTOL HOLSTER

Drastic changes took place during the middle of the 1800's. Beaver trappers found themselves out of business, many Plains Indian tribes were moving onto reservations and the old, single shot, muzzle loading rifles and pistols were history.

Personal protection offered by the new ball and cap pistols was significantly improved. The old flint lock and percussion cap pistols were usually carried by sticking them under the belt, but when the new repeating revolvers came on the market a much easier method of transportation was needed; thus the creation of the leather pistol holster.

The first ones were very simple, the only requirement was a semi-secure enclosure fastened on a belt which allowed a person to walk, ride or work without fear of loosing the weapon.

Many of these new revolvers found their way into Indian hands and they added their own personal touches and decoration to the holsters they crafted.

The holster discussed here is a reproduction of those worn by frontiersmen and scouts such as Kit Carson. Fancy carved leather and fast draw holsters came much later.

Materials Needed

2   Square feet of lightweight (4 to 6 oz.) cow hide
2   Square feet of elk or deer hide
10 Feet of sinew
    Awl and harness needle

The first step is most important. Lay the revolver on a large piece of brown wrapping paper. Use a pencil to draw the outline around the pistol as indicated in *Figure 39-1*. Be sure to provide enough room to stitch the front flap of the holster closed and extend the pattern on the handle end of the pistol to provide for a folded belt loop.

With scissors, cut out the pattern and fold it around the revolver. Remember, there will be two layers of leather; the outer leather and the elk or deer skin liner. This is done because a weapon moves a little when carried and cow hide tends to rub the blue finish off of a gun when the two come into direct contact. The soft liner serves as a cushion and protects the weapon from the cow hide cover. The pistol should fit snugly in the holster and not be too loose. This is a custom made holster and will fit no other weapon, so take plenty of time and be assured the pattern is correct before proceeding. Trim the pattern here and there as needed to assure it conforms to the weapon.

When satisfied, lay the pattern on the elk or deer skin and with a new Exacto knife, cut the inner liner. Use extreme care during the cutting process, sharp knives make nasty cuts! When completed, fold the liner over the pistol and check the fit once again. If trimming is needed, now is the time; take a little off at a time. It is much easier to trim a little several times than to cut off too much and ruin the inner liner.

Figure 39-1

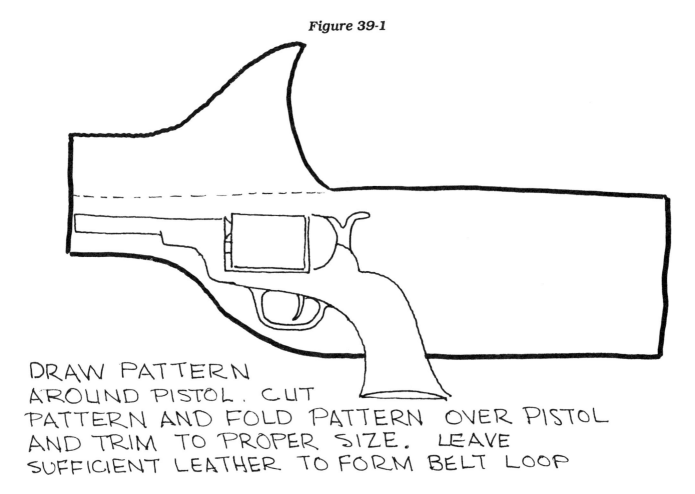

DRAW PATTERN
AROUND PISTOL. CUT
PATTERN AND FOLD PATTERN OVER PISTOL
AND TRIM TO PROPER SIZE. LEAVE
SUFFICIENT LEATHER TO FORM BELT LOOP

Next, place the cow hide on a work area, rough side up and place the inner liner, rough side down, on top of the cow leather. With a #2 pencil, trace around the liner. Remove the liner and apply a coat of rubber cement on the rough sides of the cow hide and the deer skin. When the cement becomes tacky, place the deer skin on the leather, rough sides together, and press down to form a firm bond. Using the liner as the pattern, cut away the excess cow hide. Fold the leather over the pistol and check one last time for a proper fit.

With the front of the holster folded into place, use the awl to form a line of holes completely through both sides of the holster. These holes should be spaced approximately 1/16" apart.

Use the saddle stitch to sew all edges and close the holster as indicated in *Figure 39-2*. The top and bottom of the holster are left open, but the liner must be sewn to the

SADDLE STITCH
HOLSTER WITH
SINEW

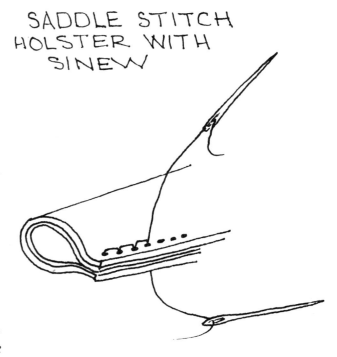

Figure 39-2

outer cover (see photograph below). Fold the belt flap over and stitch it to the back of the holster. Use the awl to make holes wherever the needle does not penetrate easily.

The craftsperson may stain the finished holster or leave it the natural color of the leather. Either way, several coats of Neatsfoot oil will help to preserve and protect the holster leather.

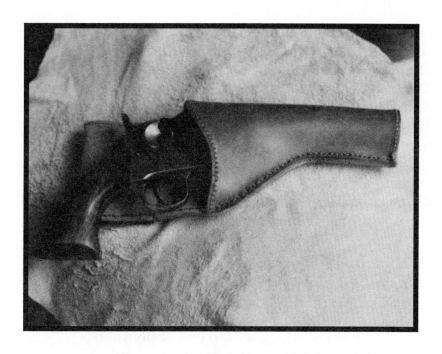

CHEYENNE COW SKULL TOTEM

Pte, the buffalo, was a sacred animal to all the Plains Indians. It was their source of life and a symbol of the abundance of Mother Earth. The buffalo provided almost everything the Indians needed to survive; rich, tasty meat to eat, robes to use for shelter and clothes, sinew for sewing, hoof and horn glue as an adhesive, bones for tools, horns for eating and drinking utensils, and the tail was used as a fly swatter. Even the skull was used as a "medicine" talisman.

In order to finally subdue the Plains Indians, the Anglos killed all the buffalo. The few remaining herds we have to enjoy today are all that remains of the tens of millions which once roamed the central plains from Canada to Mexico. A buffalo skull is nearly impossible to obtain today and if one is found for sale, the price is usually quite high.

A suitable substitute is a steer skull which when properly finished makes a magnificent wall hanging for any room.

Materials Needed

1   Steer skull
1   1/2" x 2' x 2' piece of plywood
    Paint, rabbit fur, beads and
        feathers for decoration

Steer skulls are readily available at most local meat packers and sometimes old ones can be found at garage sales or auctions. If a fresh skull is obtained, the local taxidermist has means for removing the flesh and cleaning the skull. If a large ant den is available, let nature have its way; a few weeks and the skull will be picked completely clean and the ants will be very happy! If this method is used, be sure to wire the skull to a stake in the ground or local varmints may abscond with the skull. Finish and polish the horns, first using a wood file, then ever finer grits of sand paper, finishing with #600 grit. Polish the horns with extra fine steel wool.

Cut a round back board from the plywood. For most skulls, a back board with a 24" diameter will be sufficient. Sand the back board smooth and use a good primer to seal the wood. A few hours of research at the local library will serve to locate proper designs for the skull and the back board. Each tribe had its own special designs; a few examples are given in *Figure 40-1*.

After determining the designs to be used, transfer them to the skull and back board and use flat enamel paint to complete the designs. The colors used are also important; each color signified special things. The following are some meanings for various colors:

Red	North, the people, life, war
Yellow	East, rising sun, knowledge, maturity
White	South, age, wisdom, spirits of those gone on
Black	West, thunderclouds, victory, change, strength
Green.	Earth Mother, growth, development
Blue	Grandfather Sky, the heavens

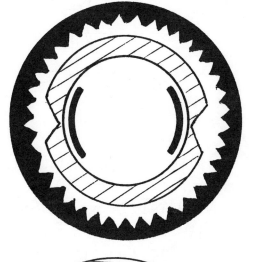

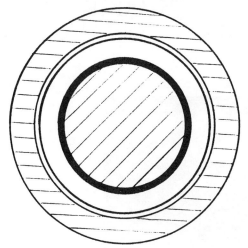

MOUNTING BOARD
DESIGNS

Figure 40-1

When the paint is completely dry, mount the skull on the board with several loops of heavy picture wire as indicated in *Figure 40-2.* All types of decorations are suitable for this talisman; feathers, beads, fur, etc. Be careful not to overdo the decoration, one or two items will be enough.

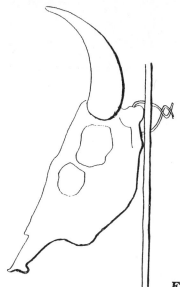

DRILL TWO HOLES IN
MOUNTING BOARD USE
HEAVY PICTURE HANGING
WIRE TO ATTACH SKULL
TO BOARD LOOP WIRE
SUFFICIENT TIMES TO
ASSURE SECURE
CONNECTION

Figure 40-2

The finished skull and back board are fairly heavy. Be sure and take this into account when preparing it for hanging. The recommended method is to drill two 1/4" holes at the top of the back board. Run a strong strip of heavy leather through these holes, as shown in *Figure 40-3*, and tie a secure knot in the ends of the strip. Use at least a 10 penny nail for hanging and be sure to drive the nail into a wall stud.

Figure 40-3

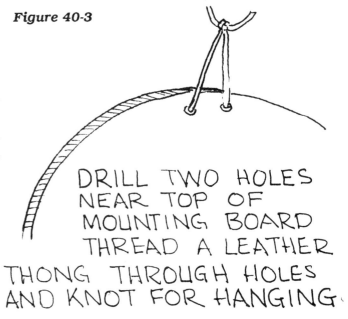

DRILL TWO HOLES
NEAR TOP OF
MOUNTING BOARD
THREAD A LEATHER
THONG THROUGH HOLES
AND KNOT FOR HANGING.

CROW PIPE-BONE BREASTPLATE

One of the most beautiful of Plains Indian artifacts is the bone breastplate. Breastplates were cherished possessions, worn only by men who fought gallantly against enemies of the tribe. Various warrior bands attributed great power or "medicine" to the breastplate and believed that it protected the one who wore it in times of fighting and war. Within some tribes, after the breastplate was completed, the band's medicine man gave special blessings to this sacred item. It was always worn by the warrior in battle and since life on the plains was subject to attack at most times, many men wore their breastplates daily.

The breastplate was made of eagle bones. The bones were carefully selected, then boiled to remove all the flesh. Each bone was carefully cut to the proper length and the marrow removed. It was then set in the sun to dry. After several weeks the bones were bleached completely white. Each bone was laced into the proper pattern by using strips of buckskin and sinew. Beads were also added to enhance the beauty and "medicine" of the breastplate.

When a warrior died, the body was washed and dressed in its finest apparel. It was then wrapped in a buffalo robe, along with many other personal items and food for the anticipated journey. The body was buried on a scaffold or tied to the branches of a tree. To assure protection from evil in the hereafter, a warrior's loved ones always made sure his breastplate was in place.

Many of the finest western museums have several of these breastplates on display. Always look for this item when visiting such exhibits as they are examples of the finest craftsmanship ever seen.

Materials Needed	
56	5/16" x 4" White pipe beads
28	5/16" x 2" White pipe beads
or	
8	36" x 5/16" pine dowels
	Sanding sealer, flat bone-white
	paint and finishing materials
3	3/8" x 36" buckskin straps
156	Black barrel beads
52	Red barrel beads
25	Yards of artificial sinew

Since eagles are protected by the federal Endangered Species Act, a substitute for the bones in the breastplate must be found. Many hobby shops and Indian trading posts have plastic or bone pipe beads for sale, and this is the first option. But due to the number of pipe beads needed for this project and the cost involved, another option is offered. This second option is to make the breastplate beads from very economical 5/16" dowel material which is well within the financial limits of most craftspeople. This project covers the use of both materials.

Regardless of the method used, it takes a great deal of time to construct this project. Some steps are repeated time after time and boredom can get the best of most crafters, causing them to get lazy and start doing poor work. Don't ruin this beautiful project by working too long at any one time. It may take as long as a month or maybe two to complete, but with loving care the finished breastplate is well worth the time involved. If boredom begins to set in, simply quit work for a while and do something else. Don't hurry this project!

If the beads are to be made from dowels, the dowels must first be cut to the proper lengths. Begin by cutting six of the pine dowels into 4" lengths. This should give 54 individual pieces. From the remaining two dowels, cut two more pieces which are 4" long (56 total) and 28 pieces, each 2" long.

The dowels must be shaped by whittling and sanding, as illustrated in *Figure 41-1*.

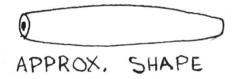

APPROX. SHAPE

Figure 41-1

Once the decision to make the beads is reached, complete the work of shaping and move on to the next step. It is difficult but not impossible to drill a hole accurately all the way through the length of the beads. Take plenty of time and be sure the drill bit is aligned with the dowel during the drilling process.

Sand each bead thoroughly and cover each one completely with sanding sealer. It is suggested that the beads be strung on a piece of thread during the sealing process (see *Figure 41-2*). This will allow the sanding sealer to dry completely and keep the beads from touching each other. After the sanding sealer has dried, sand each bead lightly with 400 grit sand paper.

Figure 41-2

Chances are each bead will have to receive three or four coats of sanding sealer before it becomes smooth enough to paint. Remember, this dowel is a substitute for smooth bone. When the craftsperson is satisfied that the grain of the wood will not show through the finish, the "bones" are ready to paint. White plastic model paint is recommended. Although there is a soft patina on dry bones, they usually don't shine like gloss paint, so be sure to use the flat finish version of the paint. A soft patina is easily added after the paint is dry by spraying the beads with a coat of semi-gloss lacquer obtained from the local hobby shop in a spray can. Don't hurry during this process - the true beauty of the breastplate comes from careful sanding and painting of each individual bone.

As soon as the bones are completely dry the breastplate is ready for final assembly. Punch 1/16" holes in two of the 3/8" buckskin straps as indicated in *Figure 41-3*. On each strap, the end that will be on the outside of the breastplate should be 16 inches longer than the piece on the inside. Notice also that a 4 inch "yoke" must be left at the top of each strap.

To begin assembly, thread sinew through the top, outside hole of one of the straps. Follow with a black barrel bead, then a 4" bone bead, and then another black barrel bead. Lace the sinew through the next strap, add a red barrel bead and a 2" bone bead, followed by another red barrel bead. Thread the sinew through the third buckskin piece, add a black barrel bead, a second 4" bone bead, another black barrel bead and go through the last strap. Add

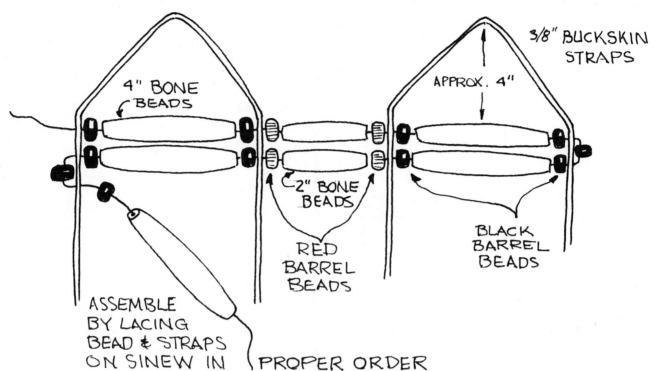

4" BONE BEADS

3/8" BUCKSKIN STRAPS

APPROX. 4"

2" BONE BEADS

RED BARREL BEADS

BLACK BARREL BEADS

ASSEMBLE BY LACING BEAD & STRAPS ON SINEW IN PROPER ORDER

Figure 41-3

another black barrel bead before lacing the sinew back through the last leather strap. Repeat the above process, back and forth across the breastplate until all of the bone beads have been strung. *Figure 41-4* shows how to add one last barrel bead and tie off the end of the sinew at both ends of the bead lacing procedure.

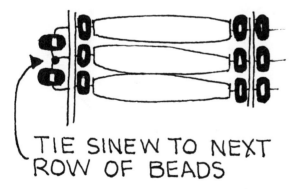

TIE SINEW TO NEXT ROW OF BEADS

Figure 41-4

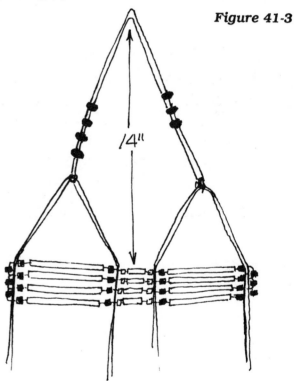

14"

TIE NECK STRAP TO THE TWO YOKES. DECORATE WITH BARREL BEADS IF DESIRED.

Figure 41-5

When the breastplate itself is finished, the neck strap is added by tying as indicated in *Figure 41-5*. The neck strap may be decorated with barrel beads, if desired.

The longer outside straps of the breastplate are used as tie straps, which go around the waist of the wearer as detailed in *Figure 41-6*.

The breastplate is now completed. Other decorations, such as feather fluffs may be added as desired. This item should be displayed in a special place. It is full of good medicine and deserves special treatment.

INSIDE STRAPS

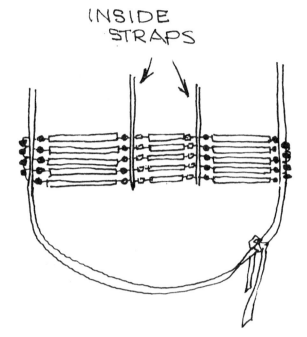

OUTSIDE STRAPS ARE 16" LONGER THAN INSIDE STRAPS. WHEN WORN, THE OUTSIDE STRAPS ARE TIED AROUND THE WAIST TO HOLD BREASTPLATE SECURELY IN PLACE.

Figure 41-6

LAKOTA WAR BONNET

Without a doubt, the Lakota Sioux war bonnet is the most attractive hat ever worn. The Sioux were the originators of the eagle-feathered war bonnet, but today it is worn by almost all tribes when they dress for ceremonies and pow-wows. It has become an Anglo symbol for all Indians; they sometimes believe an Indian without a war bonnet is hardly an Indian at all.

The Sioux used eagle feathers when crafting their war bonnets. The eagle was a sacred bird and held great mysteries. Working with the eagle feathers and making such a hat was a spiritual thing for the Sioux and the work was never rushed. It is good to make a war bonnet. There is much medicine in the feathers and it becomes good medicine for all who work with them. It has been said that one's life is never the same after making a war bonnet; it does something to the spirit.

Remember eagles are protected birds and as such must be left completely alone. If you live in one of those special places where the eagles visit, be still, watch, listen and learn from these magnificent creatures. We adopted them as the symbol of our country; respect the eagle and all that they stand for.

This project takes thirty-two feathers, sixteen curving to the right and sixteen curving to the left. All feathers should be about the same size and shape and make an attractive presentation when laid next to each other. Again, do not bother our eagle brother, use the imitation feathers found in the local hobby shop. White feathers with black tips make very attractive war bonnets, but the color should be the personal choice of the maker.

Materials Needed

32	Feathers.
96	White base fluffies
32	White tip fluffies
32	Leather Strips 1/2" x 4 1/2"
32	Pieces of felt, 1 1/2" x 2 1/2"
1	Old felt hat
	Leather strips, glue, thread seed beads

The first step is preparation of the 32 main feathers. First, each feather is "smoothed up" by fingering it from the quill to the outer edge of the feather. Feathers have a natural "zipper" which holds the feather flat; fingering will secure these zippers and make the feather very attractive. If the main feathers don't respond to fingering, a bit of steam usually takes care of the problem (see *Figure 42-1*).

Next, tie three fluffies to the base of each feather, using thread and a touch of glue as shown in *Figure 42-2*.

Fold one of the leather straps over the base of each feather and wrap snugly with thread. This leather strap must be in the same plane as the web of the feather. Leave enough space at the bottom of the folded

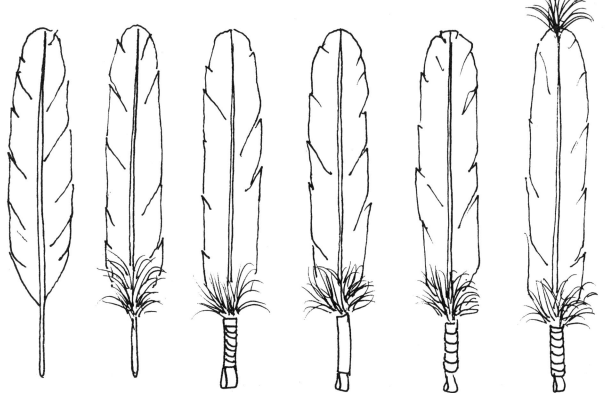

Figure 42-1   Figure 42-2   Figure 42-3   Figure 42-4   Figure 42-5   Figure 42-6

leather for another strip of leather to pass through as illustrated in *Figure 42-3*.

Wrap one of the pieces of felt around each leather strap and sew it up the back (see *Figure 42-4*).

Wrap colored thread around each felt piece for decoration, as shown in *Figure 42-5*.

Glue a fluffy on the tip of each feather (see *Figure 42-6*) and set the feathers aside in a well protected place.

The next step is constructing the foundation of the war bonnet. An old "ten-gallon" cowboy hat works very well, but any sturdy felt hat will work. Indian-craft supply companies sell hats for this purpose. The main concern is to get a sturdy one - if the foundation is too flimsy, the finished war bonnet will lose its shape and look too floppy. The hat should be large enough to allow three fingers to slip under the edge when worn on the head.

With a pair of scissors, cut the hat as shown in *Figure 42-7*. It must extend down to the eyebrows in front and down over the

back of the neck. Be sure to leave the ear coverings. The most common mistake in creating a headdress is cutting the foundation too short; better too long than too short.

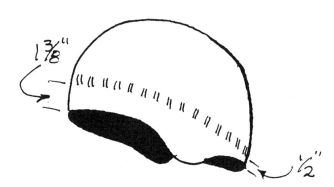

Figure 42-7

Squash the foundation flat on a work table and draw a line around the crown of the hat. To do this, first mark a point 1 3/8" from the edge at the front and mark another point 1/2" from the edge at the back. Connect these two points with a line around first one and then around the other

138

side of the hat so that the line extends all the way around the foundation.

The next step is to cut a series of slits all the way around the foundation. These slits should be 1/4" long and 1/4" apart with a 1/2" space between each pair of slits, as indicated in *Figure 42-8*.

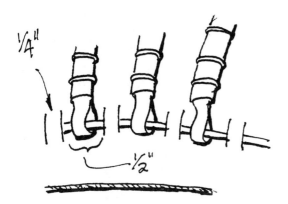

Figure 42-8

Spread the feathers out in the order in which they will be inserted on the foundation. The two longest, one right and the other left, are for the front center of the war bonnet. The remaining feathers should taper down by length around each side. Place the first two feathers on the foundation by sliding a thin leather strip through the foundation and the feather leathers as shown in *Figure 42-8* and continue until all thirty-two feathers are installed; the ends of this strip are tied at the back and the ends allowed to dangle down the back of the wearer.

The last step is placing a tie-wire through each feather to hold the feathers in place. Work on the backside and run a fine awl through each feather about 6" from the bottom of the feather. Start with one of the front feathers and run a length of fine jewelry wire through the hole. Loop the wire around the front feather and put it through the next feather, heading towards the back of the war bonnet, as shown in *Figure 42-9*. Continue until the 16th feather on that side has been secured. Then start with the other

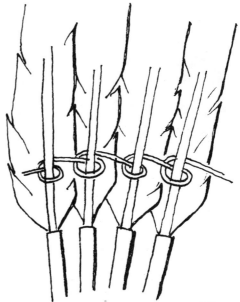

Figure 42-9

front feather and work around until the ends of the wire meet at the back. Place the headdress on someone's head and work each feather a little one way or the other to form a well balanced spread of feathers. Each feather should overlap the edge of the feather behind it. Ask the model to bend their head forward. If the headdress fails to hold its shape or turns inside out, the feathers should be shoved closer together. When satisfied with the appearance and solidity of the headdress, wind the ends of the tie wires together and clip off the excess.

A brow band must be beaded on a loom. Be sure to copy an authentic tribal design when beading the brow band - it should be 12" long and 1 3/8" wide. Sew the band on the front of the foundation, below the feather slits. The ends of the brow band are usually finished with beaded rosettes or with pieces of leather and hanging straps as shown in the picture at the end of this chapter. Some examples of rosette patterns are shown in *Figure 42-10*.

Congratulations, the Lakota War Bonnet replica is now complete. Always remember it contains strong medicine and life may never be the same after crafting this headdress. Therefore the war bonnet should be displayed in a very special place worthy of its importance and power.

BLACKFOOT   PLAINS   OKLAHOMA

Figure 42-10

HOUSEHOLD ITEMS

Contrary to average Anglo perceptions, the Plains Indians were well aware of the advantages of cleanliness and personal hygiene. True, their life style was limiting and the sanitary conditions in which they lived were primitive. But considering the life styles of most nomadic people, they were immaculate. Both sexes bathed daily, regardless of the weather. Indian women were known to change their clothes two or three times a day, whenever their clothing became soiled. They always washed their hands prior to preparing a meal and maintained a neat and orderly food preparation area. For cooking tools and utensils, they used natural materials that were available in their environment. A buffalo horn was fashioned into a fine drinking glass while part of the horn was used to make a handy spoon. The hip bone of a deer or elk made a ladle for stirring and gourds made great cups.

HORN CUP AND SPOON

Buffalo horn shells are hard to find and usually very expensive. Regular steer horns are quite suitable for this project and are readily available at local packing houses.

Materials Needed

1   Large steer horn
1   Wood piece, sized to fit horn diameter
2   Metal spoons
    Finishing materials

Use a back saw to cut the rough, large end off of the horn. This cut is made perpendicular to the axis of the horn, as shown in *Figure 43-1*. Remove all scaly material from the horn by using a wood file and carefully scraping with a sharp knife. When this is finished, sand the horn completely with ever finer grits of sand paper, finishing with #400 or #600 grit. This is hard work and takes time, but will greatly enhance the appearance of the finished drinking vessel. When satisfied with the finish, measure down the horn about three or four inches and pencil a line around the circumference (see *Figure 43-1*). Once more, use the back saw to cut this section off of the horn.

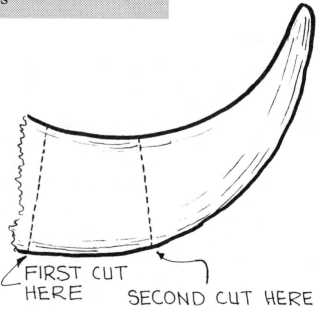

FIRST CUT HERE   SECOND CUT HERE

Figure 43-1

Fashion a round wooden plug to fit the smaller end of the cup, as illustrated in *Figure 43-2*. This plug must be slightly larger than the smaller end of the horn. File and sand the edges until they approximate the inside shape of the horn.

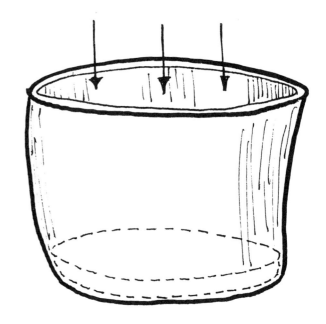

TAKE HORN OUT OF BOILING WATER, FORCE WOOD PLUG TO BOTTOM OF THE CUP. AS HORN COOLS IT SHRINKS AND FORMS A WATER-PROOF SEAL.

Figure 43-3

FASHION WOOD PLUG SLIGHTLY LARGER THAN BOTTOM OF CUP

Figure 43-2

Place the horn in a pan of boiling water and allow it to remain for about fifteen minutes. The hot water softens the shell material, making it slightly pliable. Use a pair of tongs or needle-nosed pliers to remove the cup from the water. While the horn is still hot, place the plug in the large end of the cup and force it down to seal off the smaller end, as indicated in *Figure 43-3*. Use great caution during this process, the horn will be extremely hot. Set the cup aside and allow it to cool. As the horn material dries, it will shrink around the wooden plug and form a tight, waterproof seal.

When the cup has cooled, round the top edge of the drinking vessel by scraping the outside and inside edges with a sharp knife blade. Sand the edges smooth and the horn drinking cup is finished.

Cut a spoon "blank" from the remainder of the horn, as indicated in *Figure 43-4*. Round the edges with a wood file, sharp knife blade and sand paper. When satisfied with the shape of the spoon, insert the ladle portion into boiling water for fifteen minutes.

After the material has become pliable, use tongs or a pair of pliers to remove the spoon blank from the water. Place the ladle portion of the horn spoon in a large metal cooking spoon with a smaller table spoon on top, as shown in *Figure 43-5*. Apply pressure to the two spoons with a C clamp to mold the pliable horn material into the desired shape. Again, use great care during

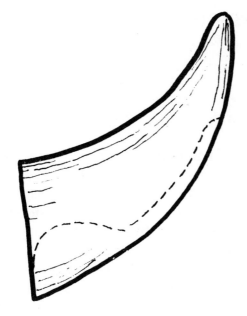

CUT SPOON BLANK FROM BOTTOM OF THE HORN THIS APPROXIMATE SHAPE

Figure 43-4

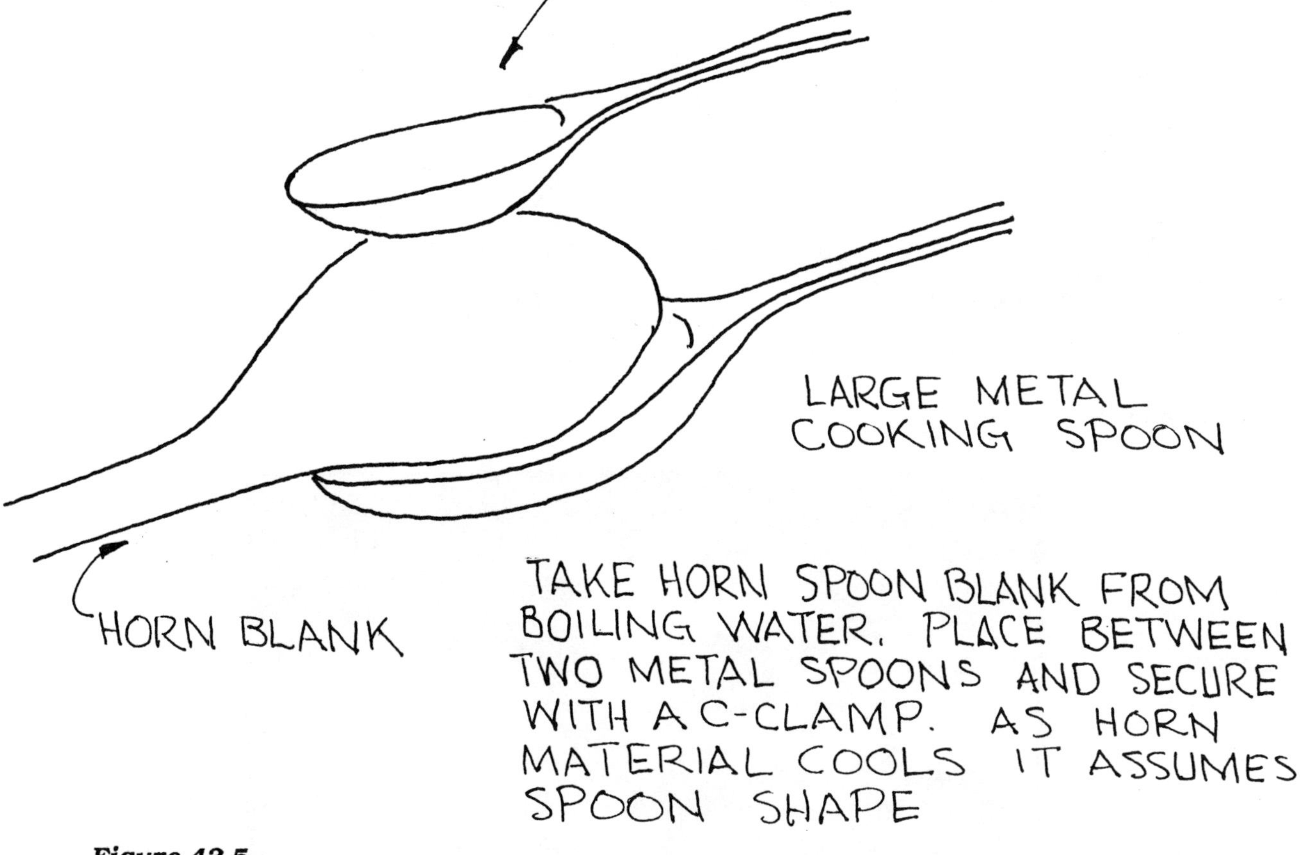

TABLE SPOON

LARGE METAL COOKING SPOON

HORN BLANK

TAKE HORN SPOON BLANK FROM BOILING WATER. PLACE BETWEEN TWO METAL SPOONS AND SECURE WITH A C-CLAMP. AS HORN MATERIAL COOLS IT ASSUMES SPOON SHAPE

Figure 43-5

this operation; the horn is extremely hot. The metal spoons must be held in this position until the horn material has cooled and assumed the new shape.

Remove the metal spoons and finish the edges of the horn spoon with sand paper.

GOURD CUP

Materials Needed

1 Gourd
   Sharp knife and metal spoon

Find a suitable gourd, preferably one with an interesting shape. Use a pencil to draw an oval on one side of the large end, as indicated in *Figure 43-6*. Use a sharp knife (a U knife is recommended) to remove this portion of the gourd.

Use a teaspoon to remove the seeds from the interior of the gourd. There are a great many seeds in there and they all must be removed. Work slowly because the outside of the gourd can be easily damaged as this operation takes place.

When all the seeds and pulp have been removed, set the gourd aside in a safe place for two or three weeks to dry. The last step is lightly sanding the edges of the oval hole and then the drinking gourd is complete.

To preserve the gourd shell, the outside of the gourd may be given three or four coats of clear varnish, if desired.

CUT HOLE IN TOP
OF GOURD
CLEAN OUT AND ALLOW
TO DRY COMPLETELY

Figure 43-6

CHEYENNE MEDICINE ARROWS

Legends are much a part of Indian culture. Each tribe has special stories of their past, some fact, some fiction, some a combination of truth and myths. Through the ages, these stories became interweaved with and eventually part of their religion. As with all religions and the strength they provide, the Indians gained great vitality from stories of their past. For people who suffered greatly from the hard times of winter and when the buffalo went away, these legends very possibly gave them the courage to survive.

One of the most interesting stories in Cheyenne culture is that of the Medicine Arrows. There are different tales of how the arrows came to the Cheyenne. Some say Motzeyouf or Arrow Boy brought them to the tribe. Others will say a young warrior called Sweet Medicine was responsible. No one can tell when this happened but all agree it was many, many years ago. As long as the tribe cared for the arrows, winters would not be too cold, buffalo would always be available to the hunters and the Cheyenne would be protected from all enemies.

Thus, the Medicine Arrows were special and sacred. A brave warrior was honored when selected by his tribe to be the Keeper of the Arrows. His responsibility was to protect the arrows at all times. To safeguard the arrows, they were wrapped in a wolf hide and placed on exhibit to the tribe only once a year; this was during the "renewal of the arrows" celebration.

There were four arrows; two red and two black. Red signified the people, black represented victory in combat. Thus the Tsis-tsistas or Cheyenne people would be safe from all misfortune as long as the arrows were properly cared for and maintained.

Among those who know, the Medicine Arrows still exist and are cared for by the Arrow Keeper of the Southern Cheyenne in Oklahoma.

No disrespect was intended when these sacred items were selected to be part of this book. On the contrary, it is with great admiration of the Cheyenne people that these special items are included. Nor should irreverence be considered in making or displaying these items. Crafters must remember that copies of very special items are being built. This should inspire the builders to read and learn more of the legends of their Indian brother.

Materials Needed

4 5/16" x 36" oak dowels
4 Arrow heads
1 Wolf hide (2 rabbit furs, sewn together
     can serve as a substitute)
    Red and black paint
    Feathers, thread, sinew, glue

The dowels should be cut 26" long. Notch one end of each dowel about 5/8" deep to accept the arrow head. Notch the other end of each dowel about 3/8" for the bow string.

Figure 44-1 gives details on this notching.

CUT NOTCH IN SHAFT ABOUT 5/8" DEEP AND WIDE ENOUGH TO ACCEPT THE ARROW HEAD

CUT A NARROW SLOT ABOUT 3/8" DEEP BUT ONLY WIDE ENOUGH FOR THE BOW STRING TO EASILY SLIDE IN AND OUT OF THE SLOT

Figure 44-1

Use flat, red paint on two of the dowels and flat, black paint on the other two. Plastic model paints are recommended and be sure to use the type that dries without any shine. The Indians used natural substances to make their paints and these dried with a flat finish. Using gloss paint shows everyone the necessary homework was not done by the crafter.

SECURE ARROW HEAD TO SHAFT WITH TIGHTLY WRAPPED SINEW

Figure 44-2

Insert the arrow heads into the notches made for them and wrap the end of each shaft with sinew as shown in *Figure 44-2*. If wrapped tightly, this bond will hold the arrow head to the shaft quite securely.

Carefully split a feather down the center of the quill with a sharp Exacto knife, as illustrated in *Figure 44-3*. Take plenty of time and great care with this operation, as these blades can make nasty cuts in fingers!

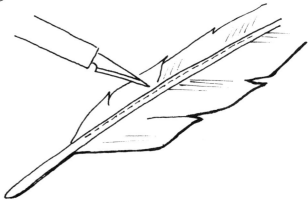

Figure 44-3

Trim the feathers as indicated in *Figure 44-4*, leaving a section of bare quill on each end.

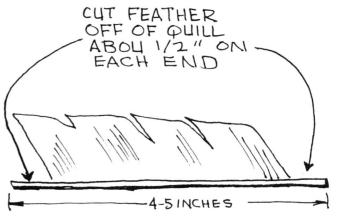

CUT FEATHER OFF OF QUILL ABOU 1/2 " ON EACH END

4-5 INCHES

Figure 44-4

Use fast drying model airplane glue to adhere the feathers to the shaft. A few straight pins help keep the feathers in place until the glue dries (see *Figure 44-5*). When the glue dries, wrap the quill ends with thread and then coat the thread with glue.

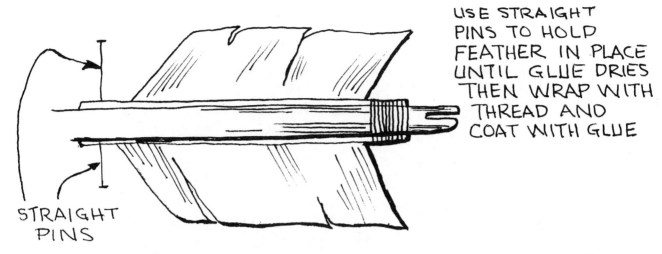

USE STRAIGHT PINS TO HOLD FEATHER IN PLACE UNTIL GLUE DRIES THEN WRAP WITH THREAD AND COAT WITH GLUE

STRAIGHT PINS

Figure 44-5

Normally three feathers are attached to an arrow, however the Medicine Arrows had only two.

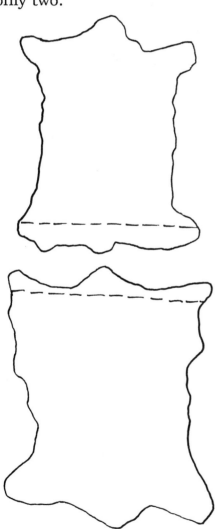

CUT ENDS OFF OF RABBIT FURS AND STITCH THEM TOGETHER TO FORM A PELT — MATCHING FURS MAKE THE MOST ATTRACTIVE COVER — WRAP AROUND THE MEDICINE ARROWS AND TIE WITH TWO THONGS.

If a wolf hide is available, it should be used to wrap and protect the arrows. Two rabbit furs, cut and sewn together as detailed in *Figure 44-6*, make a good substitute. The bundle is then secured with a couple of wrappings of leather thongs.

Always remember the religious significance of the Medicine Arrow. To the Anglo they are merely arrows; to the Cheyenne, they are the source of life itself. Treat these replicas accordingly!

Figure 44-6

147

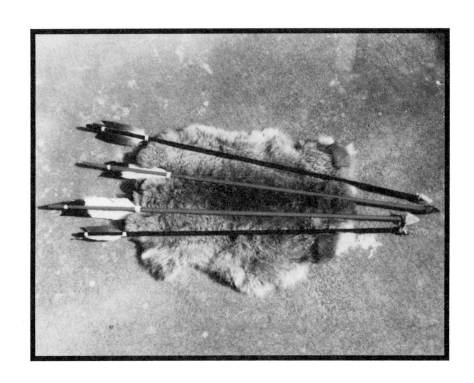

ARAPAHO SADDLE

During buffalo hunts and warfare, no saddle was used; instead a brave tied himself on his horse's back with a strap of rawhide. After mounting a horse, the rawhide was placed around the horse's girth, over the brave's bent knees and tied as tightly as possible. This strap gave little comfort, but held the brave firmly on the horse's back

The single rein, fourteen to sixteen feet long, was gathered in loops and held in the warrior's mouth with the end tied around the warrior's ankle. If the rider should fall from his horse, the rein stopped the horse from running away.

The rider changed directions by simply applying pressure on one side or the other of the horse's shoulders with his knees.

This gave the warrior complete freedom of both hands and arms during the hunt and in combat. It was not unusual for attacking warriors to slide over to one side and shoot an arrow under the horse's neck with only a foot showing over the horse's back. All this was done while the horse was running at top speed!

But contrary to popular belief, several Indian tribes made and used saddles. *Figure 45-1* shows two types of Indian saddles. These items were used for special occasions and were usually adorned with fringe, bead work or brass tacks. Most museums displaying Indian artifacts have examples of this craft.

Figure 45-1

INDIAN PAD SADDLE

FORK OF MULE DEER ANTLER OR TREE LIMB WITH RAWHIDE COVER

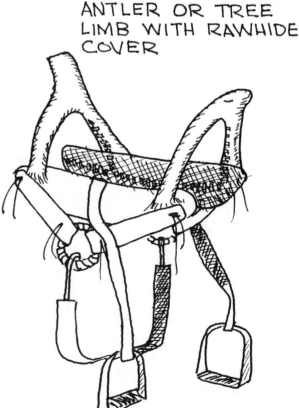

INDIAN FRAME SADDLE

149

The Indian saddle is a difficult project to build and takes a lot of study to design and construct. The instructions for the entire project must be read and digested before any work is begun. This project is not recommended for the faint of heart, but when the saddle is complete, it makes a very unusual addition to any collection. *Figure 45-2* illustrates the various components of the Arapaho saddle.

COMPONENTS OF THE ARAPAHO SADDLE

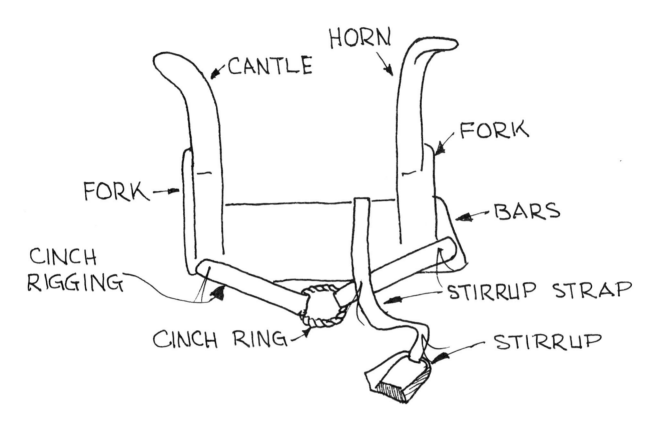

Figure 45-2

Materials Needed
1   1 x 12 x 36 inch clear, white pine
2   Stirrups
2   3" rings
Buckskin or leather
Rawhide *or* fiberglass cloth & resin
Brass dome headed tacks
Wrapping paper
Wood glue, wood filler and paint

By today's standards the Indian saddle is a primitive device, but a great deal of research is required before this project should be attempted. It may help to travel to a museum to study and photograph (for future study and reference) the saddles on display. Be sure to have a good understanding of how the saddle should look

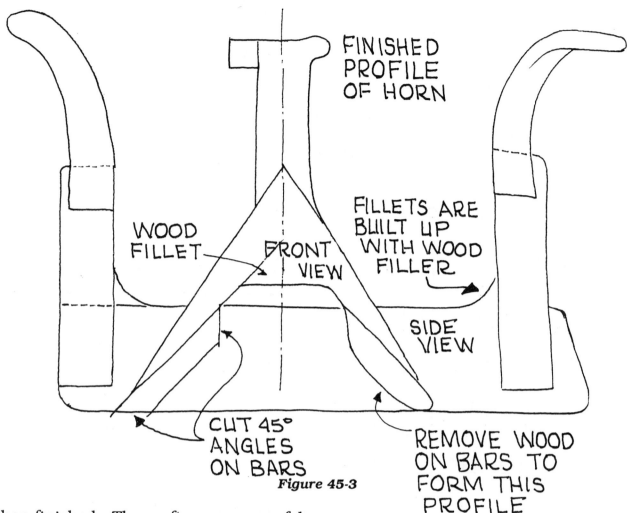

FINISHED PROFILE OF HORN

WOOD FILLET

FRONT VIEW

FILLETS ARE BUILT UP WITH WOOD FILLER

SIDE VIEW

CUT 45° ANGLES ON BARS

REMOVE WOOD ON BARS TO FORM THIS PROFILE

Figure 45-3

when finished. The craftsperson may follow the drawings presented or create an original set of drawings.

Care must be taken when purchasing the wood. Be sure it is completely flat; warped wood is almost impossible to work into this project.

To begin, use wrapping paper and draw full size patterns of all the wood components shown in *Figure 45-3*. The front and rear forks are identical; each is made of six pieces of wood - four fork pieces and two fillets, as illustrated in *Figure 45-4*. *Figure 45-5* shows details of the two bars (foundation pieces of the saddle). Note that the edges of the bars are cut at a 45° angle for later rounding into the required profile. The shape and number of horn and cantle pieces are itemized in *Figure 45-6*. When the patterns are complete, transfer them to the pine material.

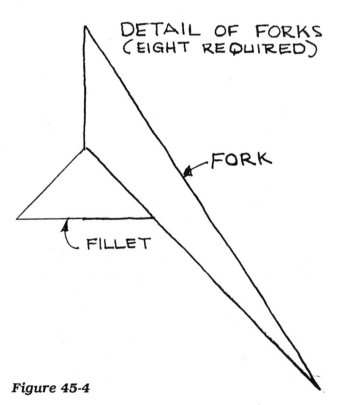

DETAIL OF FORKS (EIGHT REQUIRED)

FORK

FILLET

Figure 45-4

151

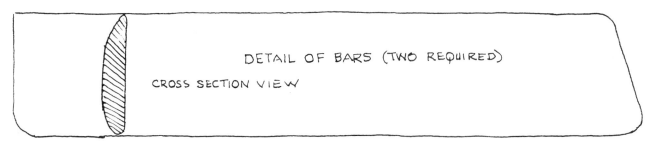

DETAIL OF BARS (TWO REQUIRED)

CROSS SECTION VIEW

Figure 45-5

DETAILS OF CANTLE AND HORN ASSEMBLIES

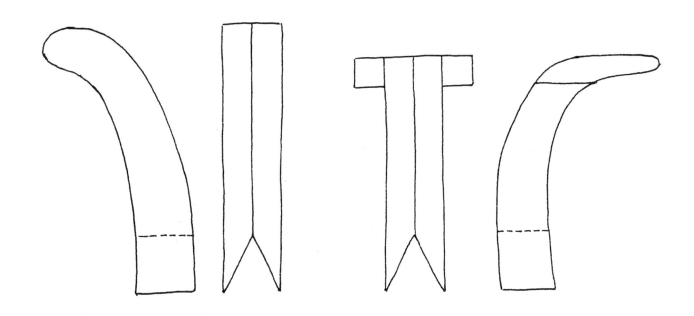

CUT TWO PIECES OF 3/4"
STOCK TO MAKE CANTLE
FORM KNOTCH TO ACCEPT
THE REAR FORK — GLUE
TOGETHER AND SET ASIDE
TO DRY

CUT TWO PIECES OF 3/4" STOCK
TO MAKE HORN — CUT KNOTCH TO
ACCEPT FRONT FORK — GLUE
TOGETHER AND ADD SMALL BLOCK
ON EACH SIDE TO FORM ROUNDED
SHAPE OF HORN TOP

Figure 45-6

Carefully, use a jig saw or a band saw with a 1/8" blade to cut out the components. Assemble the forks as indicated in *Figure 45-7* and the horn and cantle as detailed in *Figure 45-6*. Use a good wood adhesive to glue these pieces together and set them aside overnight to dry.

Attach the forks to the bars with glue and two wood screws through each leg as shown in *Figure 45-8*. Next glue the horn and cantle to the forks with a good coating of adhesive, as directed in *Figure 45-9*. Be sure to keep all the components aligned properly during assembly.

When the adhesive has dried, use wood filler in the areas indicated in *Figure 45-10*. The back of a teaspoon makes a dandy trowel to press and smooth the wood filler into the designated areas. Let the wood filler dry overnight. The basic saddle tree is

DETAIL OF FORK ASSEMBLY
(TWO REQUIRED)

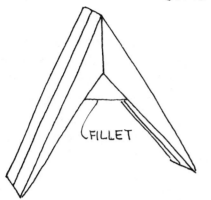

FILLET

USE GOOD ADHESIVE
TO ASSEMBLE THE FOUR
SECTIONS OF THE FORK
ADD WOOD FILLETS AND
SET ASIDE TO DRY

Figure 45-7

HORN/CANTLE ASSEMBLY TO FORK

AFTER GLUE HAS DRIED ON ALL
SUB ASSEMBLIES COAT PEAK
OF FORK WITH GLUE AND
FIT THE HORN IN PLACE ON
THE FORK — BE SURE IT IS
PROPERLY ALIGNED THEN SET
ASIDE TO DRY. REPEAT
PROCESS WITH CANTLE AND
FORK.

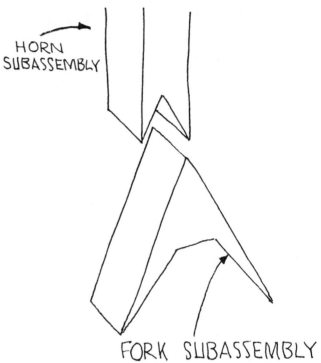

HORN
SUBASSEMBLY

FORK SUBASSEMBLY

Figure 45-9

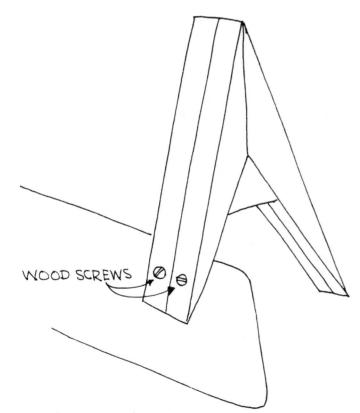

WOOD SCREWS

GLUE & SCREW
ASSEMBLED FORKS
TO BARS

Figure 45-8

USE WOOD FILLER
TO BUILD FILLETS
WHERE FORKS
ATTACH TO BARS.
THE BACK OF A
TEASPOON WORKS
WELL AS A TROWEL.

Figure 45-10

now complete.

When the adhesive and wood filler are set and cured, carefully round all the edges of the saddle tree as illustrated in *Figure 45-11*. A Dremel tool with a coarse sanding drum works great for this step, it's safer than a pocket knife and much faster. Remove a small amount of wood at a time, stopping frequently to check the progress; removing too much wood may ruin the project. Blend the wood-filled areas into the lines of the wood. The transition from filler to wood should form graceful lines.

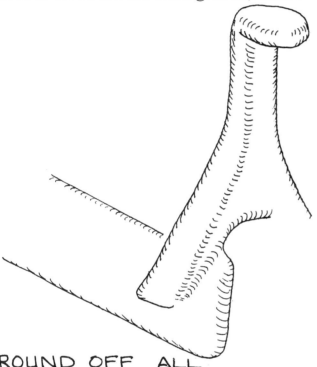

ROUND OFF ALL
SHARP CORNERS WITH
KNIFE OR DREMEL TOOL
FEATHER IN ALL WOOD
FILLED AREAS TO
FORM SMOOTH AND
EVEN LINES
Figure 45-11

When satisfied with the overall appearance of the wood rounding step, sand the entire tree with 200 grit sand paper. It is not necessary to "finish" sand the tree, as it will be covered by rawhide or fiberglass.

A bare, wooden saddle tree is pretty fragile; assurance of the integrity and sturdiness of the finished saddle comes from the next step. Indians stitched wet, green rawhide tightly to the frame to give it the necessary strength. When wet, the rawhide stretches and forms around curved surfaces and is easy to sew. When dry, rawhide forms a hard, long lasting and durable cover for the tree. This sewing process takes a lot of time and a tremendous amount of patience. A fresh hide may not be available to the crafter when needed, so it is recommended that the rawhide be replaced with fiber glass cloth and resin.

If the craftsperson prefers the fiber glass option, read and follow the instructions provided when these materials are purchased. Due to the varying shapes of individual trees, there are no instructions given here as to the right or wrong way to cover a tree. Study the shape of the tree, take plenty of time and do what appears to be correct. The end result will probably be most satisfying. Pay no attention to critics, very few people in the world have ever constructed an Arapaho saddle - be the expert!

If the tree is covered with fiber glass cloth, the resin should be tinted to resemble the color of rawhide. The crafter may desire to wait until the fiber glass has cured and then paint the tree with rawhide colored paint.

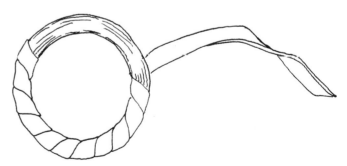

WRAP CINCH RINGS WITH
1/2" WIDE STRIP OF BUCK-
SKIN. GLUE BUCKSKIN TO
RING AS IT IS WRAPPED.

Figure 45-12

CINCH RIGGING

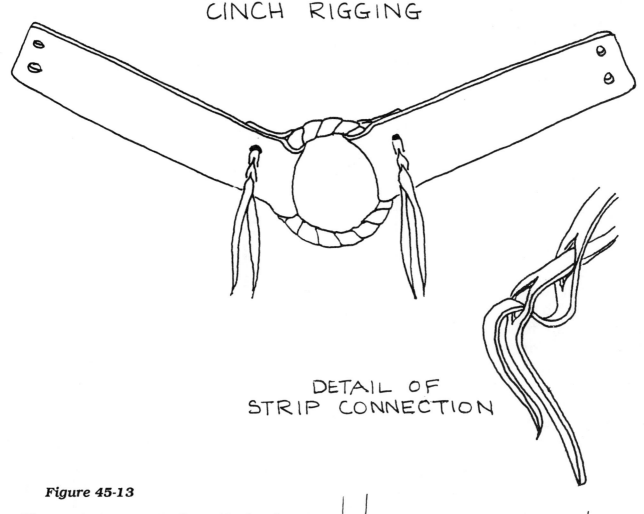

DETAIL OF
STRIP CONNECTION

Figure 45-13

The next step is attaching the leather to the tree. Cut a 1/2" wide strap of buckskin and wrap each ring as shown in *Figure 45-12.*

Cut another strap of buckskin which is 1 1/2" wide. Construct two cinch riggings as indicated in *Figure 45-13* . Attach the riggings to the saddle bars, as detailed in *Figure 45-14.*

Stirrups are difficult to construct. The author purchased the ones used in the chapter photograph from a local saddle shop. Indians used many materials in their attempts to construct stirrups, but found the most reliable ones could be obtained from Anglo traders. Stirrups should be decorated with brass tacks and fringe. Cut two leather straps, 1 1/2" wide for the stirrup straps. Attach a stirrup to one end

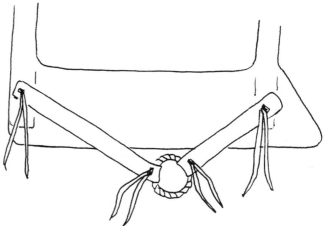

DRILL TWO 1/4" HOLES THROUGH THE FORKS AND BARS, THEN ATTACH CINCH RIGGING WITH BUCKSKIN OR LEATHER STRIPS.

Figure 45-14

of each strap and connect the other ends around the saddle bars. Use the same method to secure the straps as was used for the cinch rigging (see detail in Figure 45-13).

SPECIAL NOTE: This project is for display only. Do not attempt to use this saddle on a horse. It is most uncomfortable for a human to ride; it is not strong enough to support a person's weight unless made with rawhide; and it is extremely hard on the back of a horse. If desired, build a wall mounted saddle horse, as shown in Figure 45-15. Find a nice wall in the den, attach the saddle horse with a couple of lag bolts and display this new prize with pride!

SADDLE RACK
(all measurements approximate)

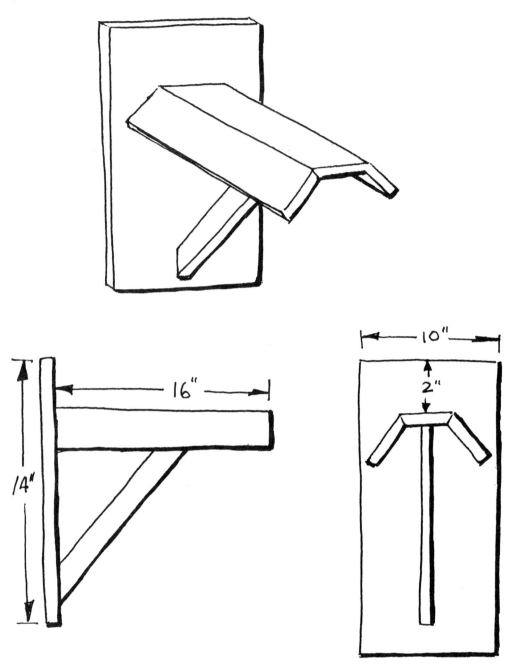

Figure 45-15

Congratulations, a most difficult project has just been completed. As one of the very few Indian saddle builders in the United States, take pride in this accomplishment!

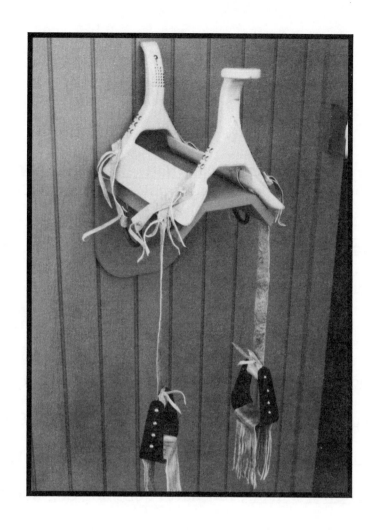

REFERENCES

Amsden, Charles A., Navaho Weaving, University of New Mexico, Albuquerque, 1949.

Bryon, Nonabah G. and Young, Stella, Navaho Native Dyes, Indian Handcraft Series Number 2, Education Division, United States Office of Indian Affairs, Washington, D.C., 1940.

Clemens, J.B., Dream Catcher, Catalog No. 5 Lietzau Taxidermy, Minnesota.

Eagles, Steven, Spirit Catchers, Catalog, NY, 1989.

Ewers, John C., The Blackfeet, Raiders of the Northwestern Plains, University of Oklahoma Press, Norman, OK 1958.

Grant, Bruce, American Indians Yesterday and Today, E.P. Dutton & Co., 1958.

Hunt, W. Ben, Indian Craft, Bruce Publishing Co., Milwaukee, 1942.

Lowie, Robert H., Indians of the Plains, McGraw-Hill, New York, 1954.

Lowie, Robert H., The Crow Indians, Rinehart Publishing Co., New York, 1935.

Mason, Bernard S., The Book of Indian-Crafts and Costumes, A.S. Barnes & Company, 1946.

TECHNIQUES OF NORTH AMERICAN INDIAN BEADWORK

by Monte Smith

This informative, easy to read book contains complete instructions on every facet of doing beadwork. Included is information on selecting beads; materials and their use; designs; making a loom and doing loomwork; applique stitches such as the lazy, "crow", running, spot and return stitches; bead wrapping and peyote stitch; making rosettes and beaded necklaces; and beadwork edging. There is a section of notes, a selected bibliography and an index. The book features examples and photos of beadwork from 1835 to the present time from 23 tribes. Anyone interested in Native American craftwork will profit from owning this book.

HOW TO TAN SKINS THE INDIAN WAY

by Evard H. Gibby

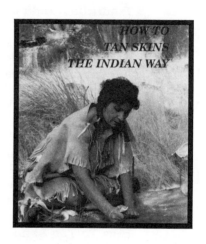

This exciting edition includes everything you need to know to make attractive, functional leather and skins, at a fraction of the cost of buying them. The brain tanning method used by American Indians is described in clear, simple terms and the text is augmented by illustrations and pictures of all the techniques and tools described. Included are: tanning rabbit and sheep skins with the hair on, making flannel soft buckskin, smoking hides, and making rabbit skin ropes and blankets. This book will be invaluable to anyone interested in traditional skills of the American Indian.

TRADITIONAL INDIAN CRAFTS

by Monte Smith

This book includes complete, illustrated instructions on all the basics of Leather, Bone and Feather crafts of the American Indian. Projects include: Bear Claw Necklace, Sioux Dancing Choker, Quilled Medicine Wheels, Feathered Dance Whistle, Double-Trailer Warbonnet and much more. In addition, craft techniques described include quill wrapping, shaping feathers, how to size projects, using imitation sinew, how to antique bone, obtaining a "finished" look and hints on personalizing craft projects. Designed so that even beginners can create authentic Indian crafts with ease.

HOW TO MAKE PRIMITIVE POTTERY

by Evard H. Gibby

Learn how to find naturally occurring clay, make a pot from this clay, fire it successfully, and use it to cook in a primitive setting. Noted author, Evard Gibby leads the reader on an exciting exploration of the techniques for making attractive, functional earthenware. There are more than 60 photos which show each step in the pottery-making process, plus many finished items. Included are sections on Clay Preparation, Tempering Clay, Finish and Decoration, Primitive Firing, Other Objects made from Clay, and more. A great book for those interested in primitive skills and for those who like to make their own craftwork!